MIND'S EYE

An Eye of the Beholder Collection

PETER KUPER

Dedicated to
any similarity between persons living or dead
(which is purely coincidental).

Mind's Eye
© 1997, 1998, 1999, and 2000 by Peter Kuper. All rights reserved.
ISBN 1-56163-259-7

All of the strips in this book were originally published in *Funny Times*, *The Nation*,
The Progressive, *In these Times*, *Comic Relief*, *Tucson Weekly*, *Pitch Weekly*, *Austin Chronicle*,
The Alibi, *The New York Daily News*, and *World War 3 Illustrated*, among others.

Also available in this series:
Eye of the Beholder, $10.95

Designer: Peter Kuper
Production: Laird Ogden
Thanks to Steven Heller and Tom Bodkin at *The New York Times* for getting the "Eye" ball
rolling, Ray and Sue at *Funny Times* for being the first to pick it up, all the papers that keep me
drawing every week and Katherine, Paul and Laird for their invaluable work on this collection.

Published by NBM
555 8th Ave. Ste. 1202
New York, NY 10018
www.nbmpublishing.com

5 4 3 2 1
Printed in China

ComicsLit is an imprint
and trademark of

NBM

NANTIER ○ BEALL ○ MINOUSTCHINE
Publishing inc.
new york

INTRODUCTION

by Andy Partridge

Peter Kuper's art is a bit like a black hole, an ink black hole to be precise.
Just like a black hole, it sucks you in, eyes first, then just when you get a grip of
what's happening, it spits you out into a totally different reality. There you are,
five panels later, in another universe, going "WOW! How did I get here? I didn't
think I would come out in this place." But you're glad you did. And the second
you stop laughing, I bet you can't wait to jump into another black hole.

You won't always laugh, though. Sometimes, Peter's art is a little bomb that goes
off in your head leaving you in the rubble of your expectation with a tart lemon
poignancy or the brusque slap in the face of disgust at human behavior.

The template he works with here in "Mind's Eye" is very original. A little journey
of four frames, leading you on with their charming linocut-like immediacy.
Then as you turn that page, POW! His sugar sweet punch comes out of nowhere.
I'll tell you one thing, if Mad had found Peter's format back in the 50's, 60's, 70's,
people would have said"Yeah, that was the best thing about that magazine!"
But they didn't, and he did.
Tough luck, Mr. Gaines.

Peter's work is very modern. It's cityscapes, taxi cabs, guns, drugs and folly.
But I've a feeling primitive man would be drawn along by the wordless vigor
and scratchy mummery of it all. It's timeless. It's a zoetrope with clout.
It's a silent film short from inside your guilty conscience.
It's the lavatory wall drawings of the gods.

Andy Partridge
Swindon, England
2000

Andy Partridge is a singer-songwriter in the band XTC.

Mind's Eye presents you with four panels of clues to guess which point of view your eyes are following. The answer to each puzzle is in the fifth and final panel on the following page...

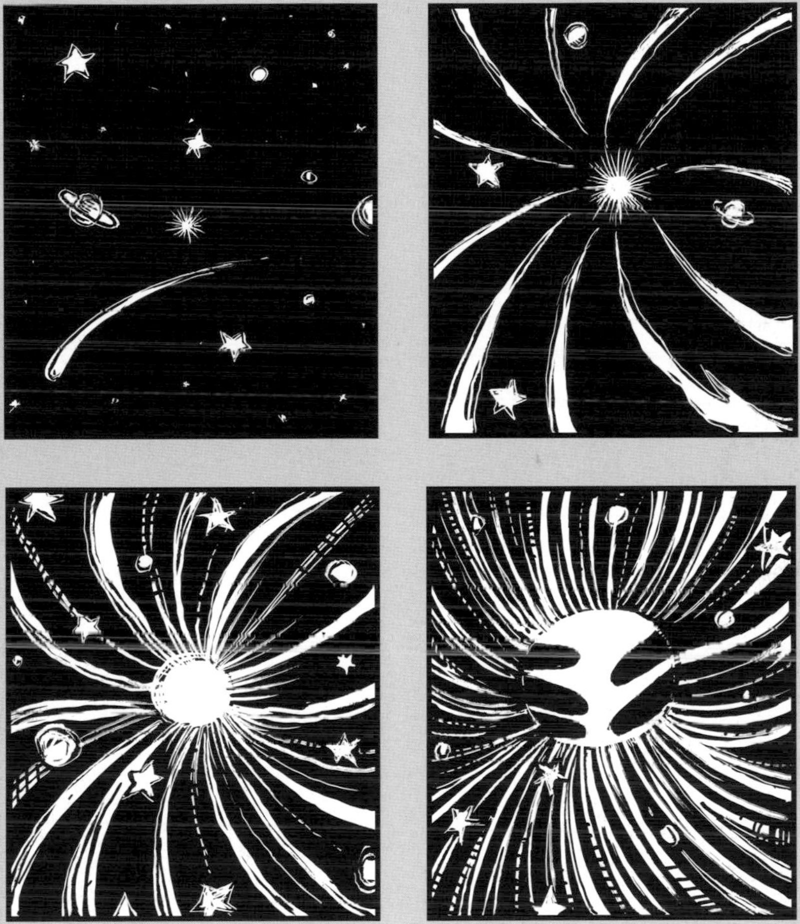

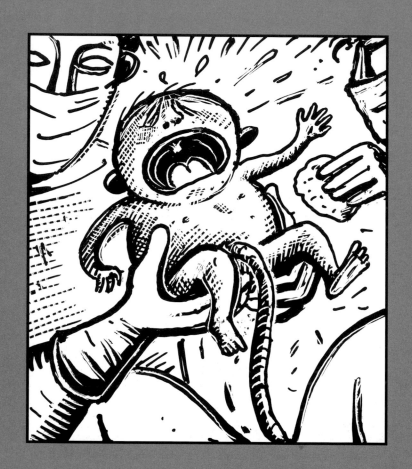

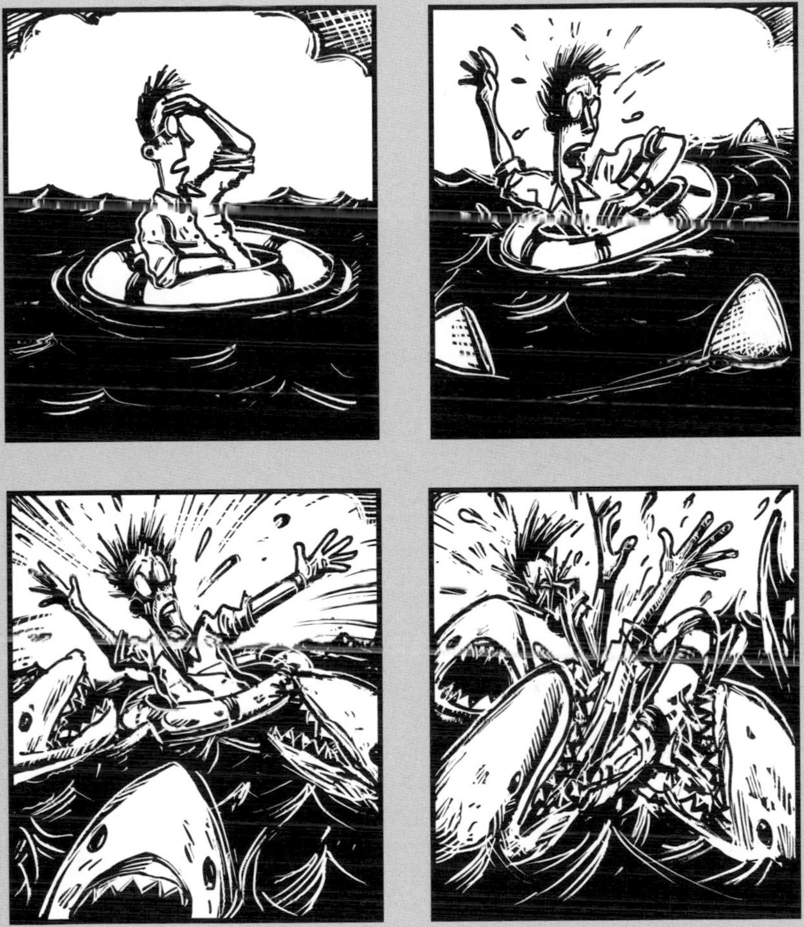

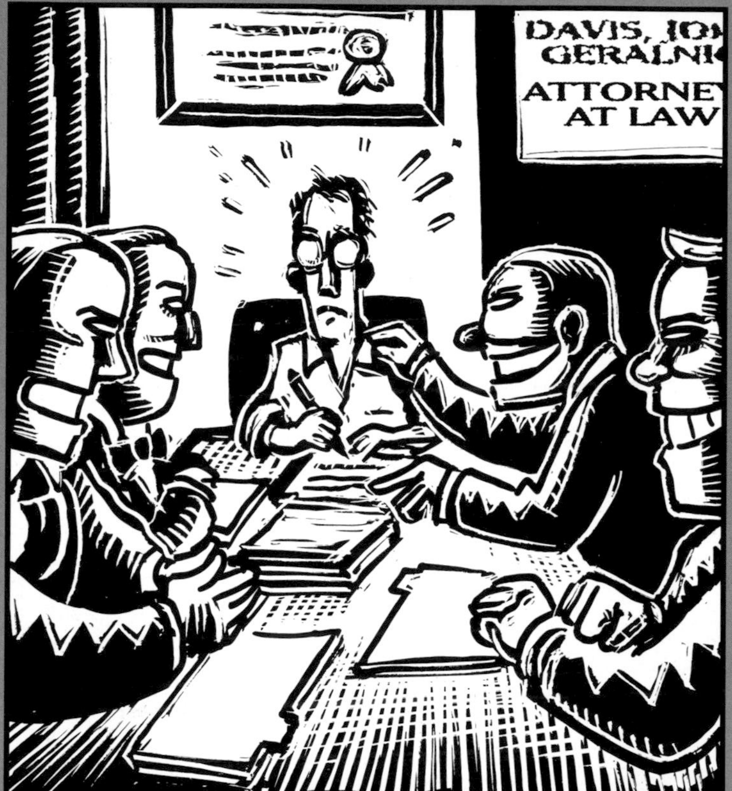
DAVIS, JO
GERALNI
ATTORNE
AT LAW

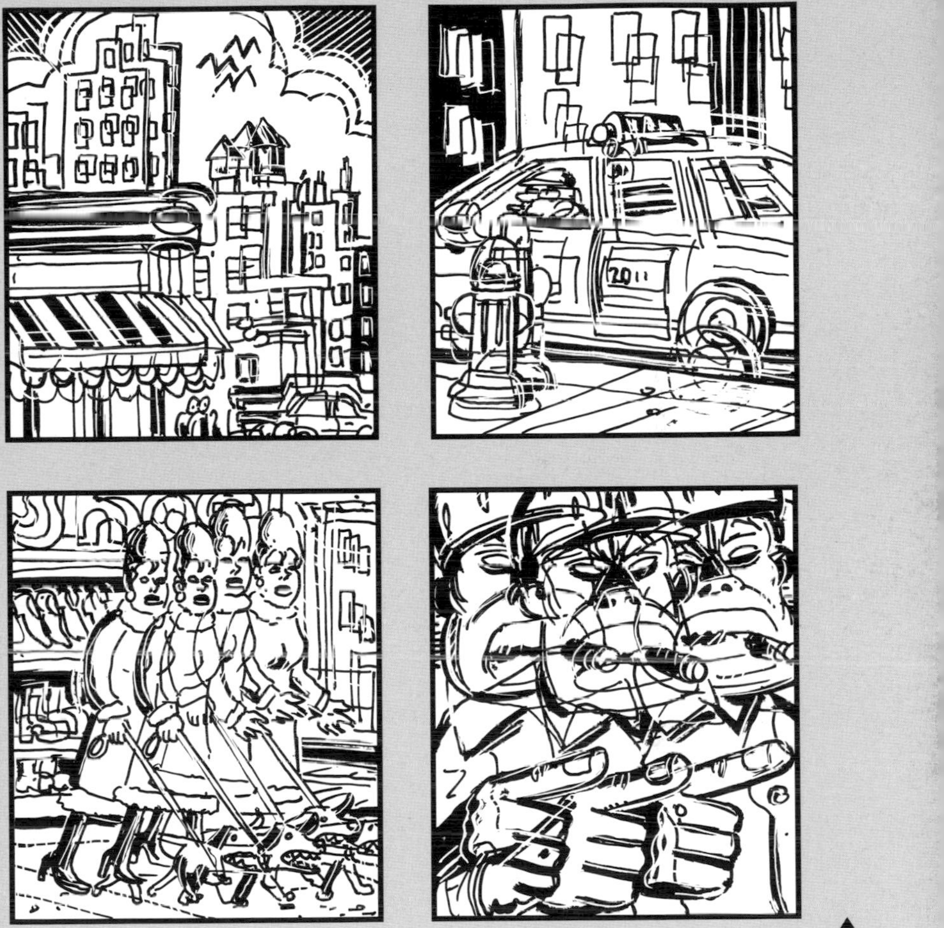

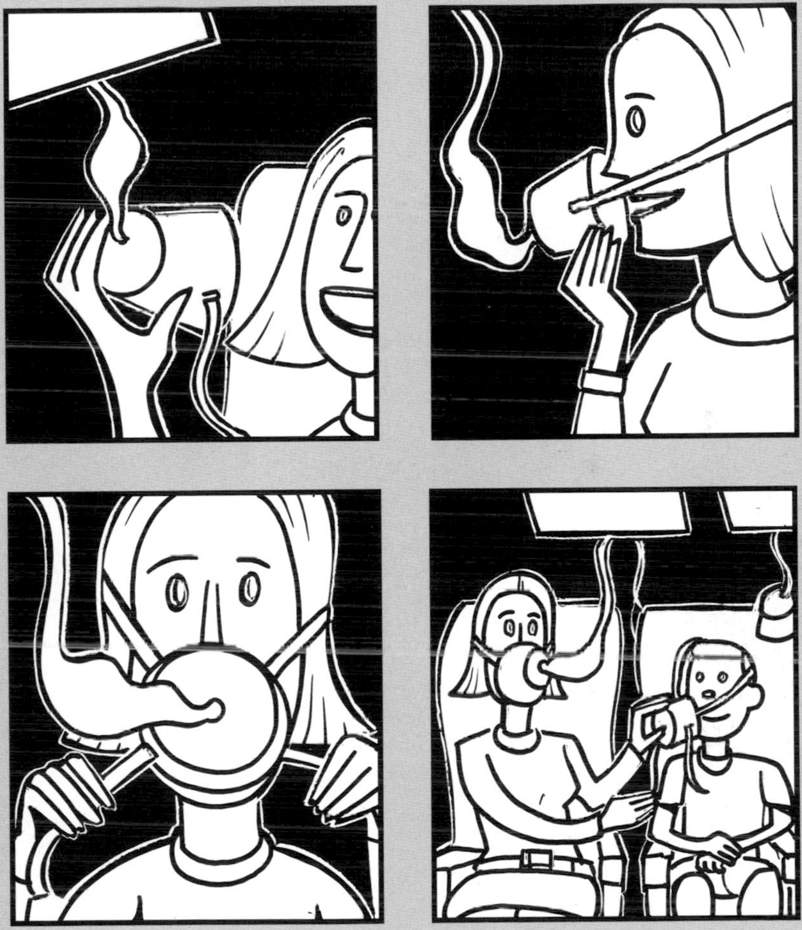

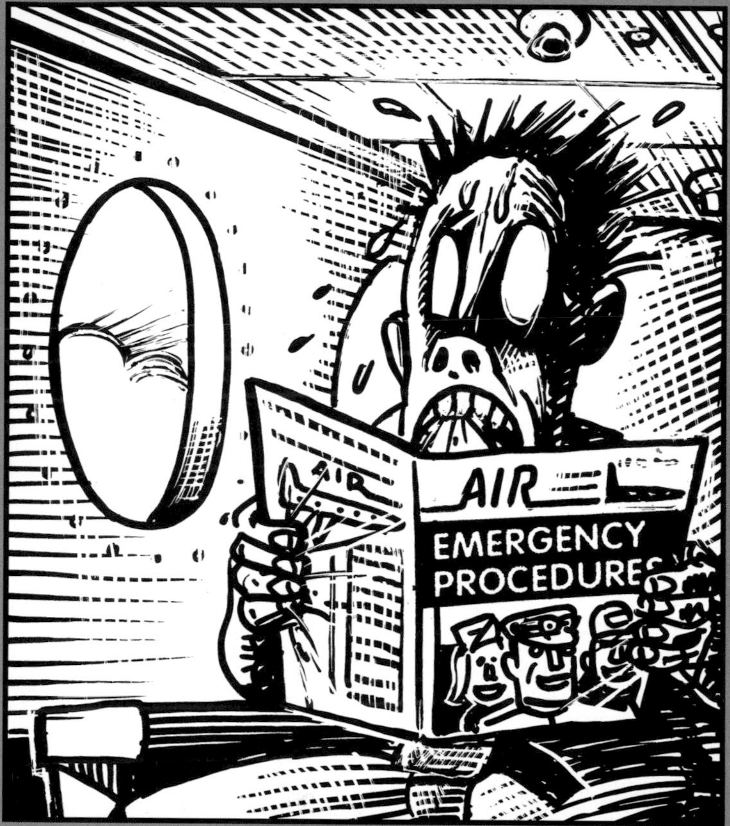
AIR
EMERGENCY
PROCEDURE

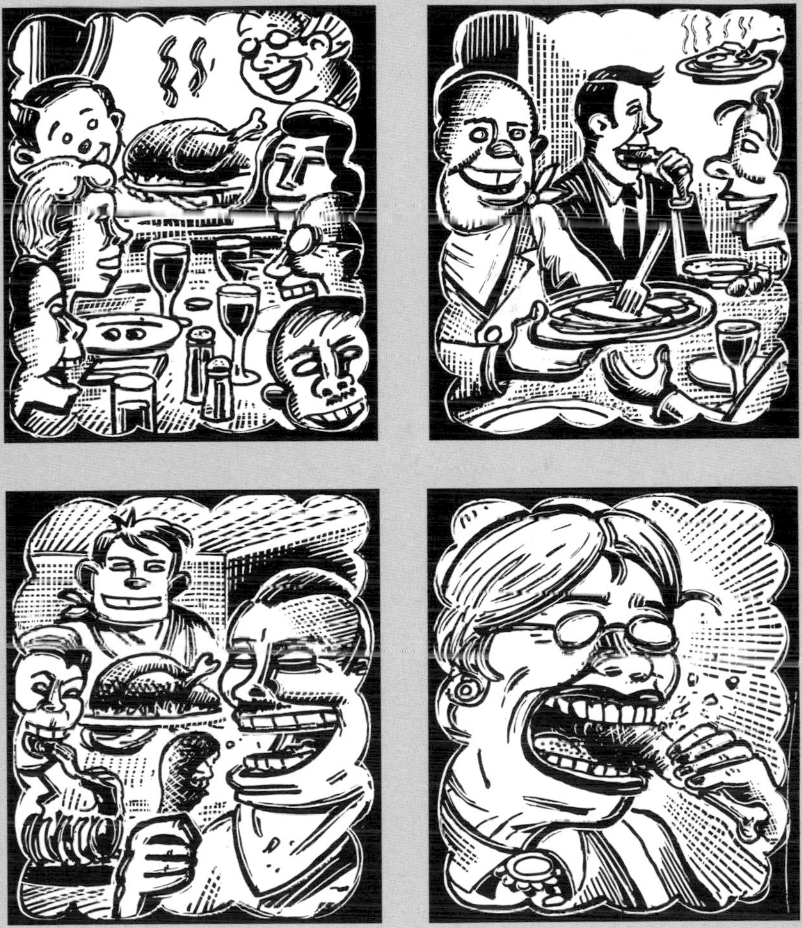

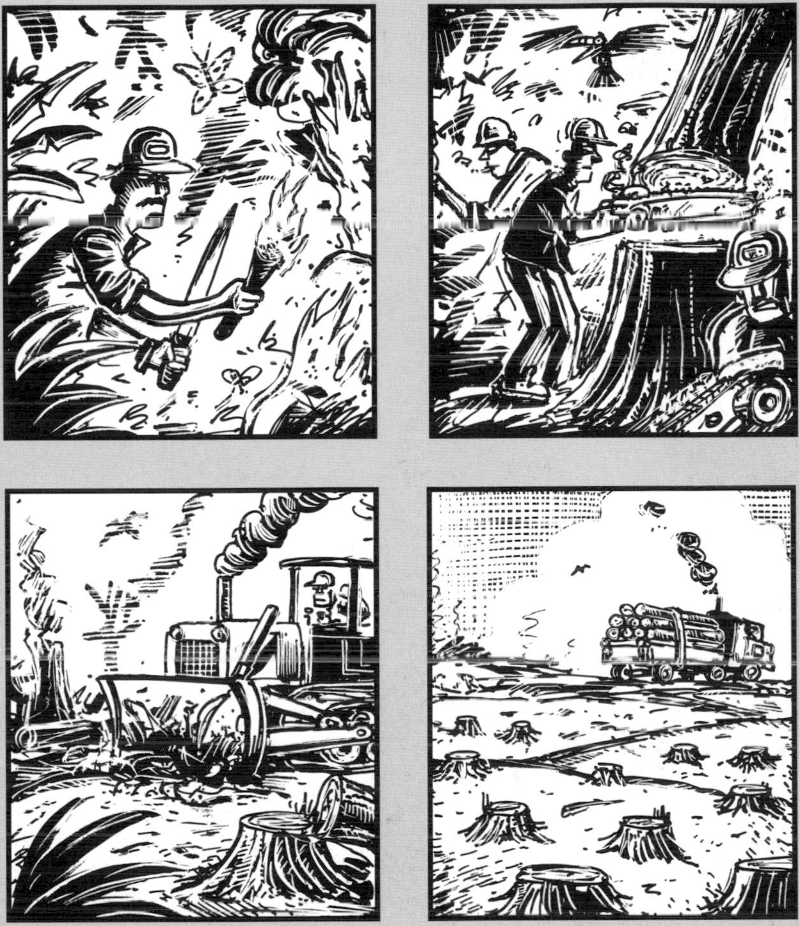

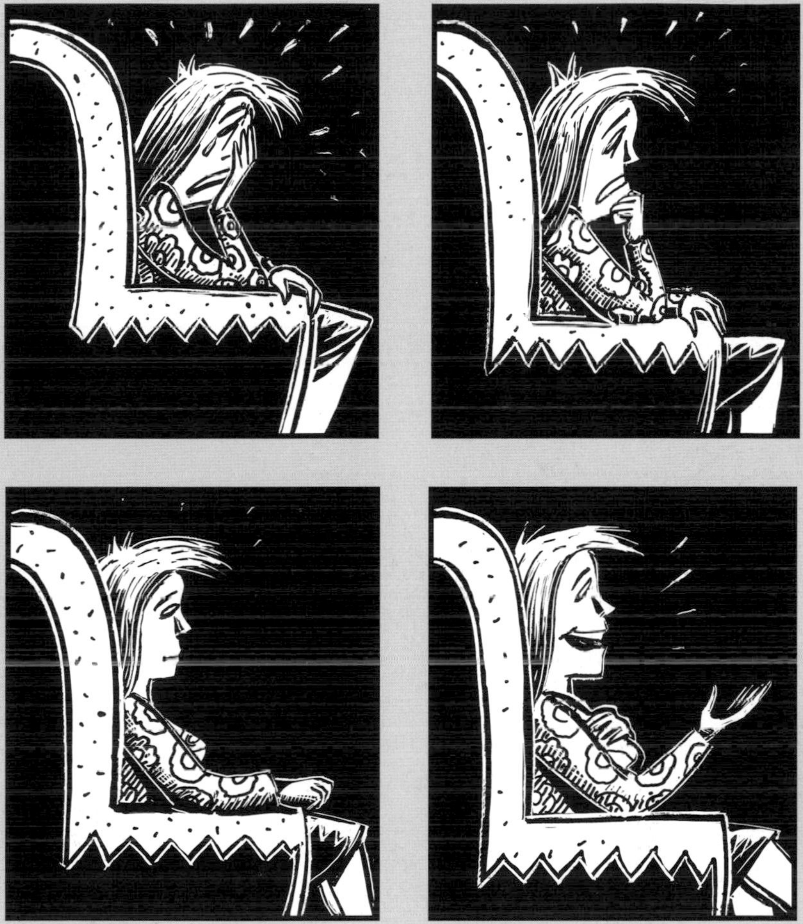

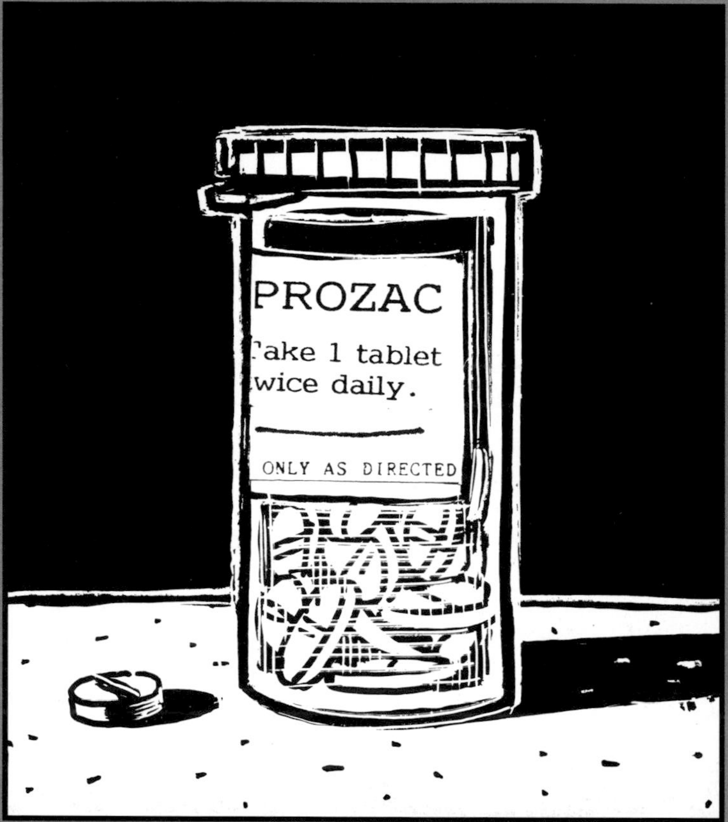
PROZAC
'ake 1 tablet
wice daily.
ONLY AS DIRECTED

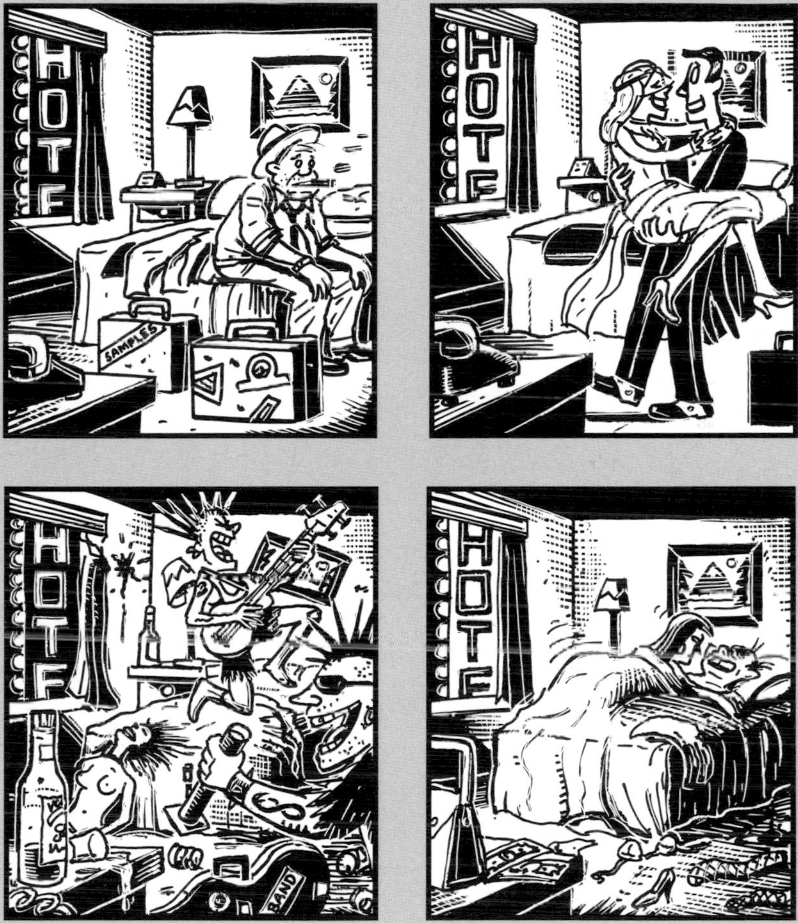
SAMPLES
BAND

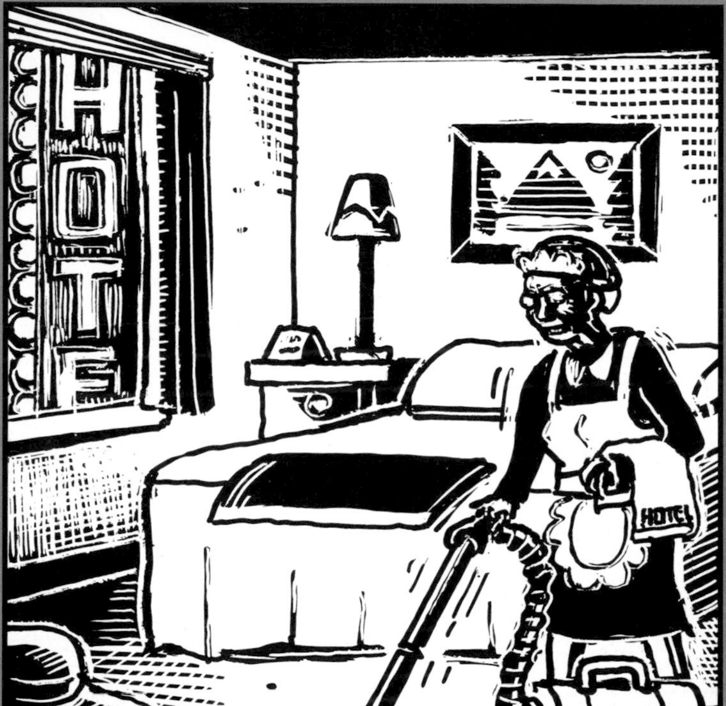
HOTEL

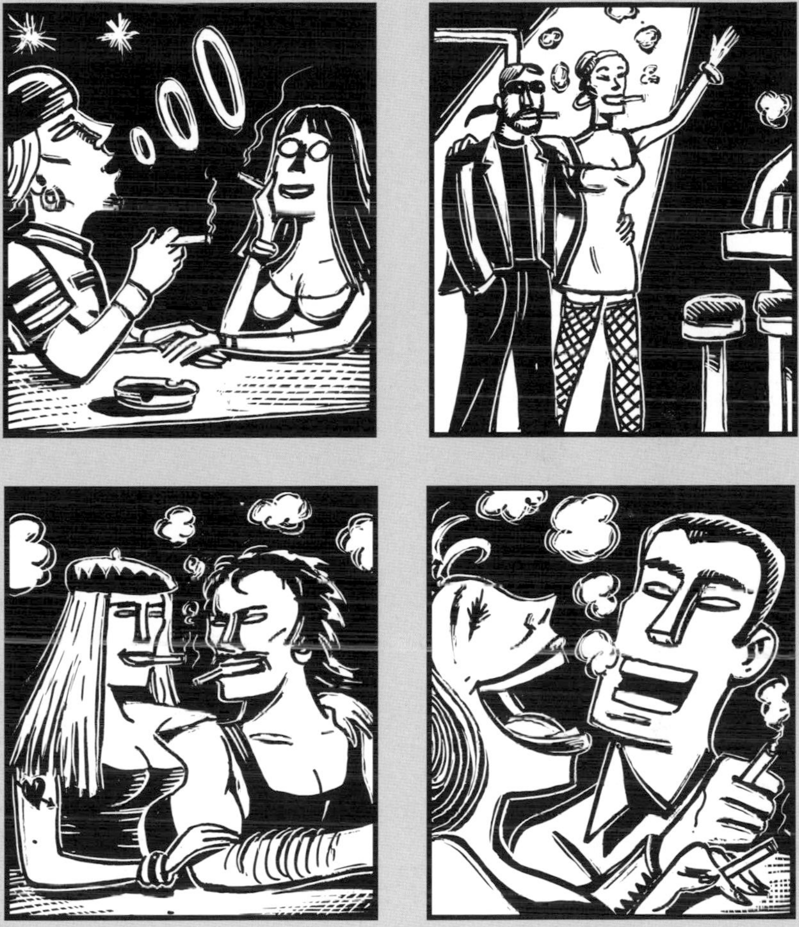

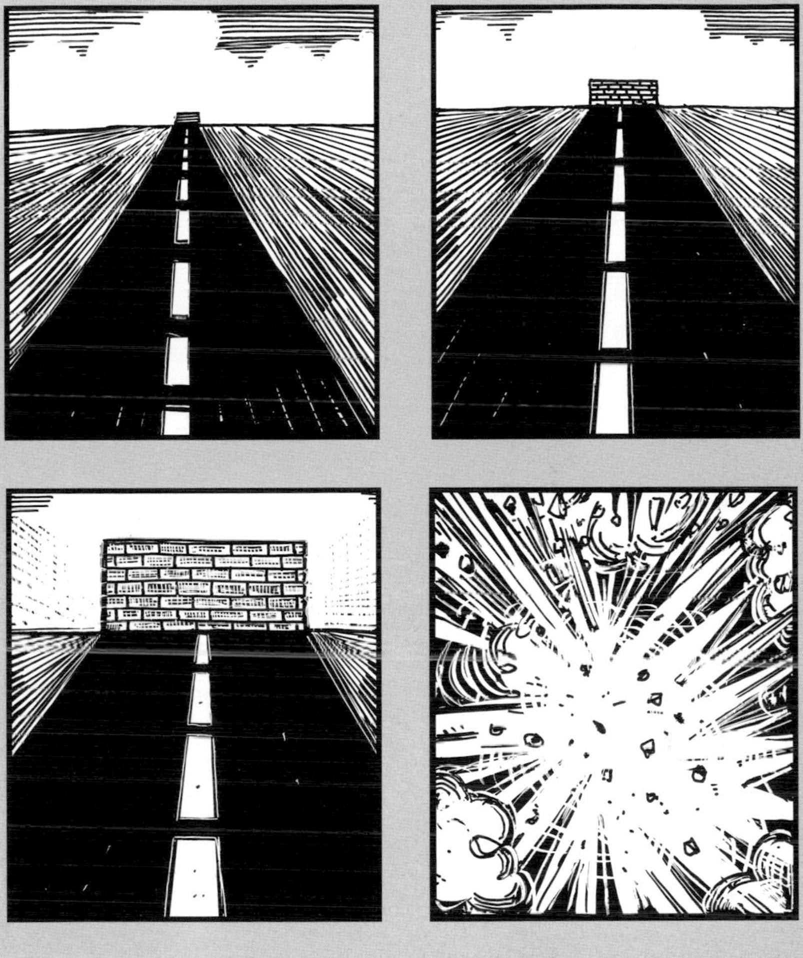

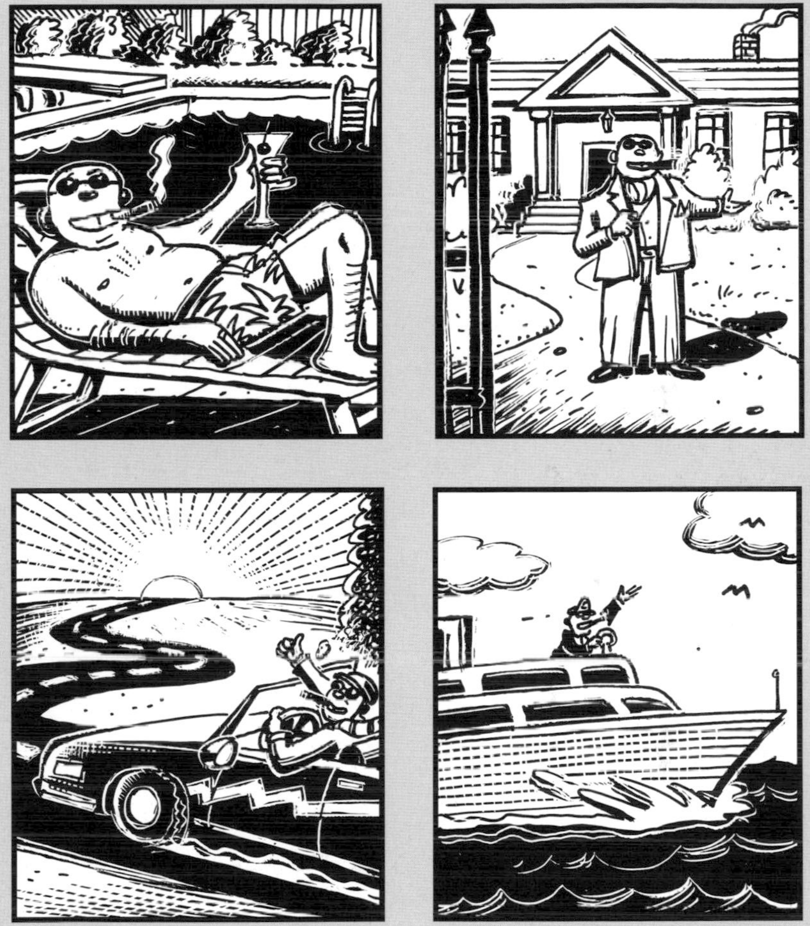

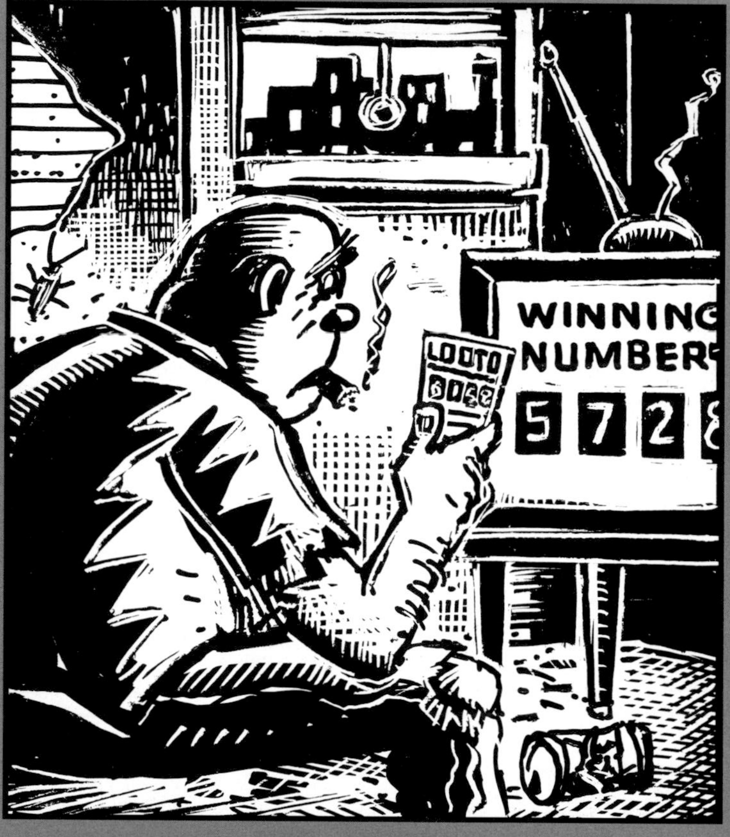
WINNING
NUMBERS
5 7 2 8

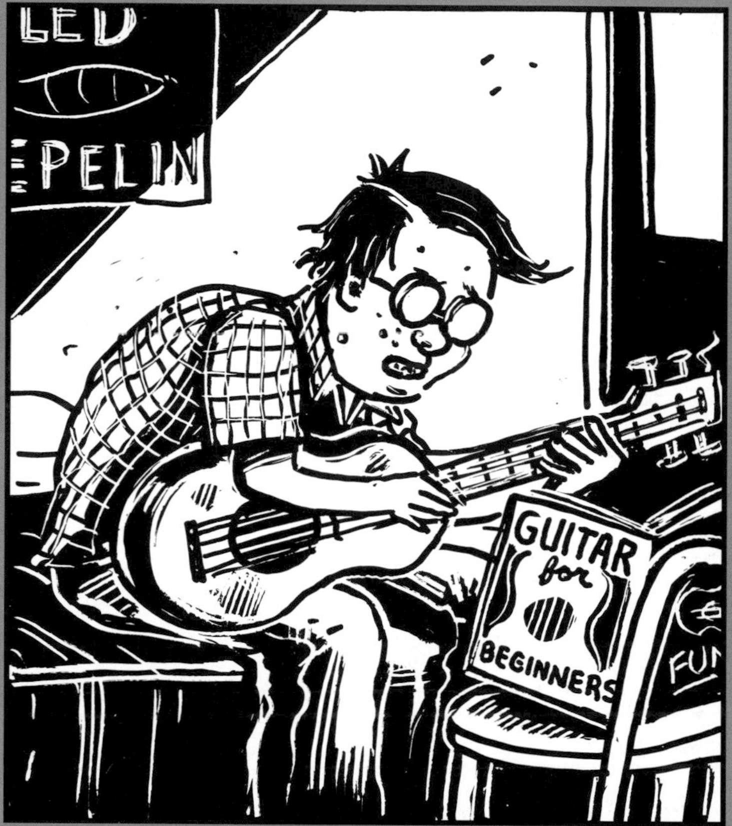
LED
EPELIN
GUITAR for BEGINNERS

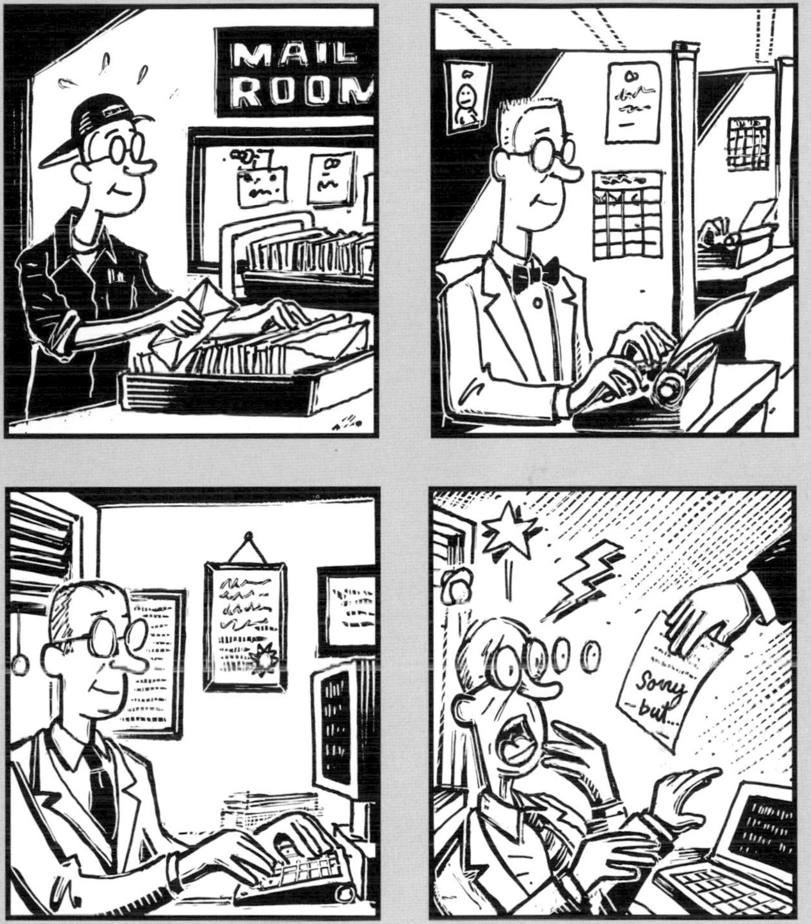
MAIL
ROOM
Sorry
but...

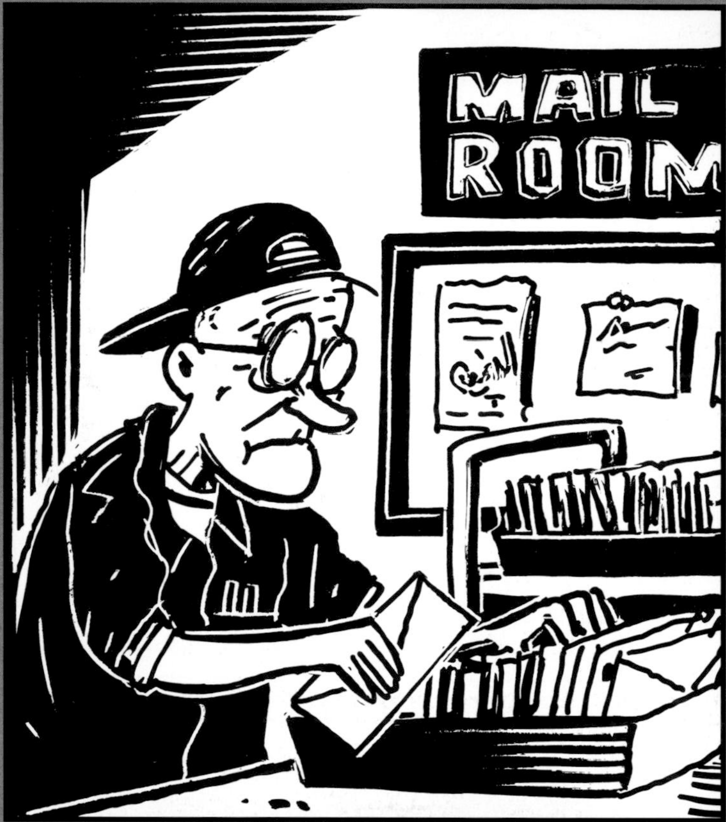
MAIL
ROOM

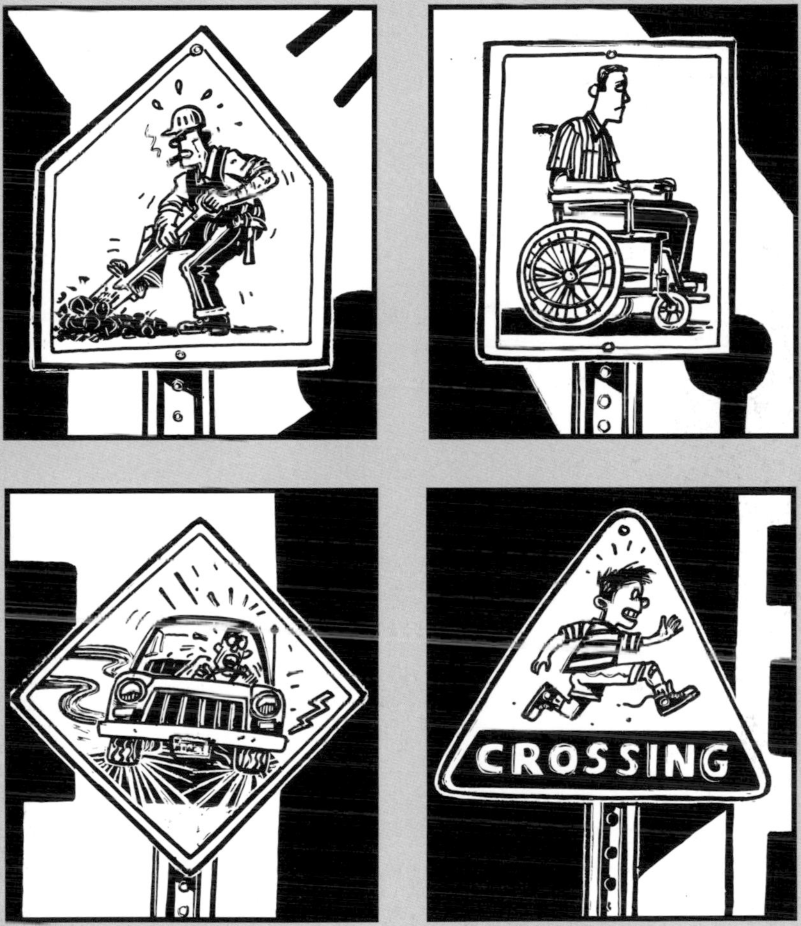
CROSSING

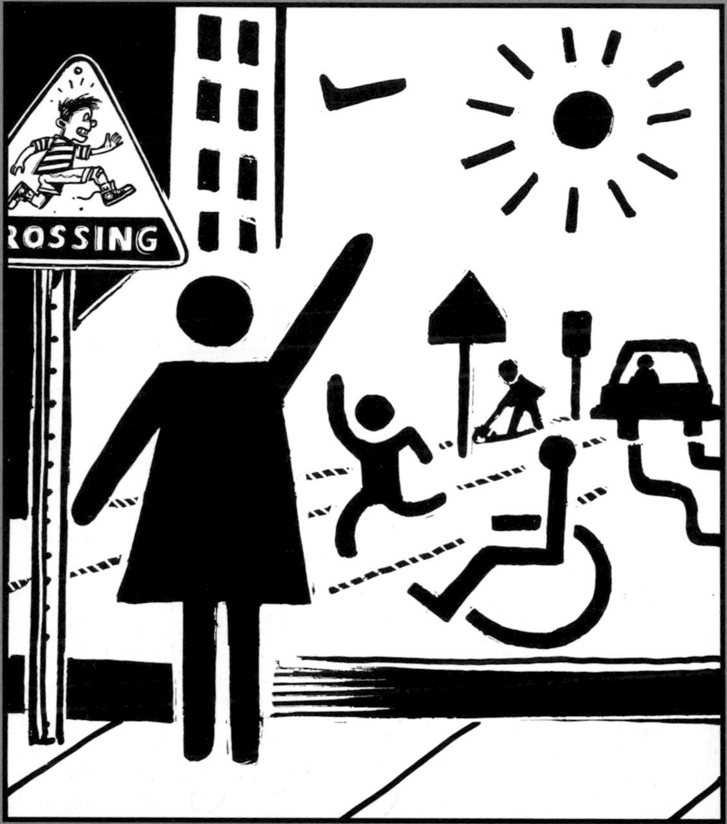
ROSSING

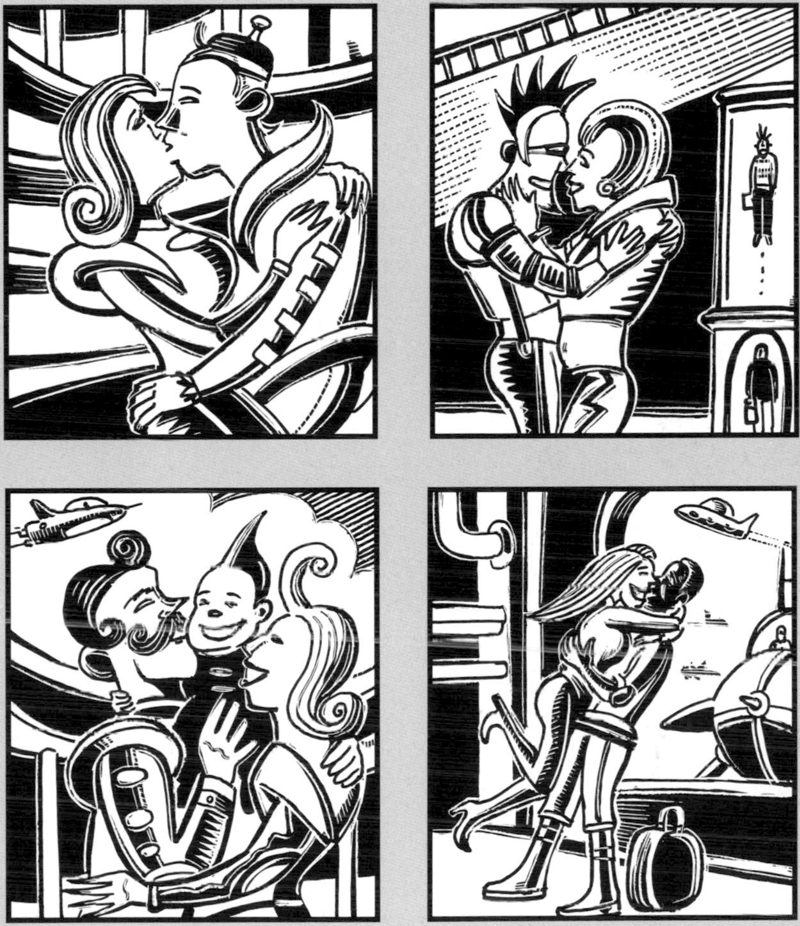

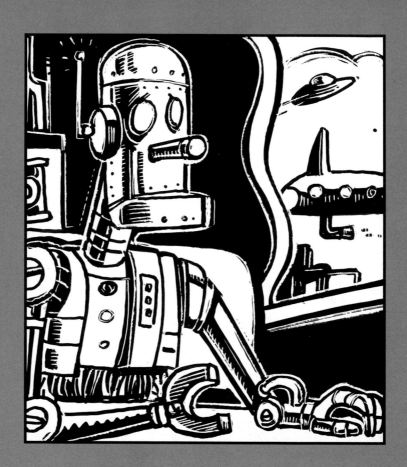

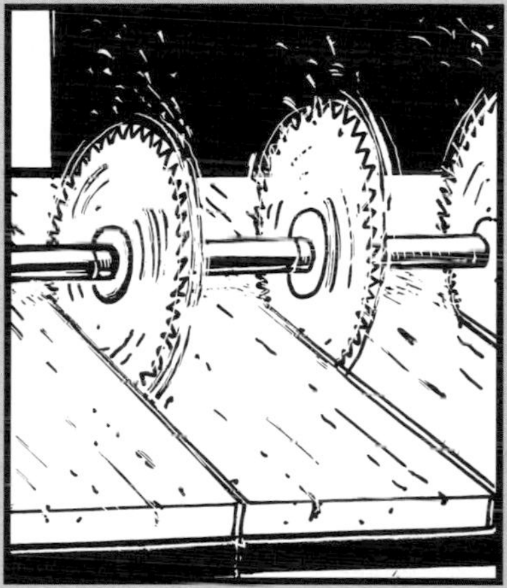

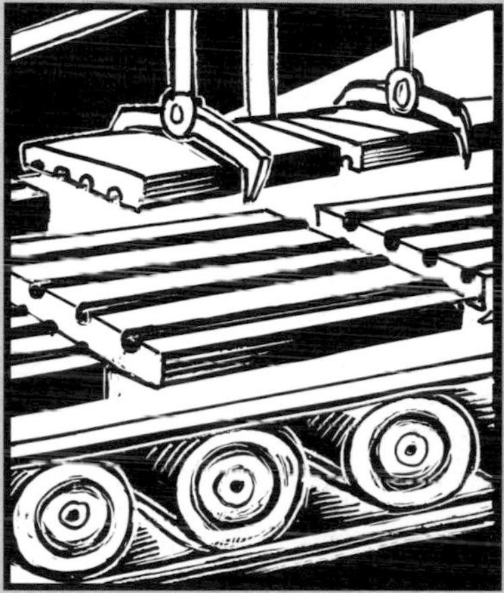

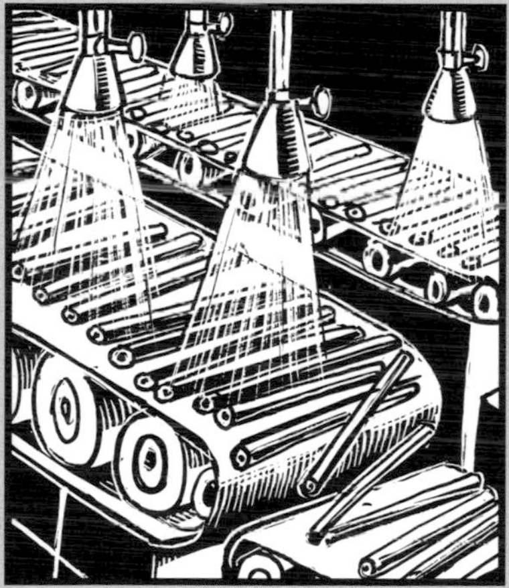

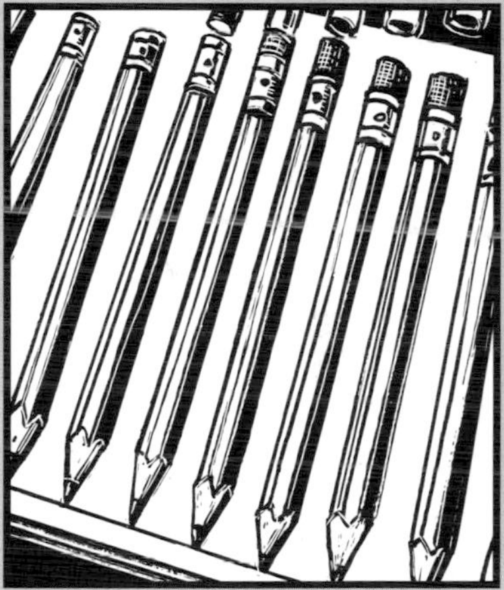

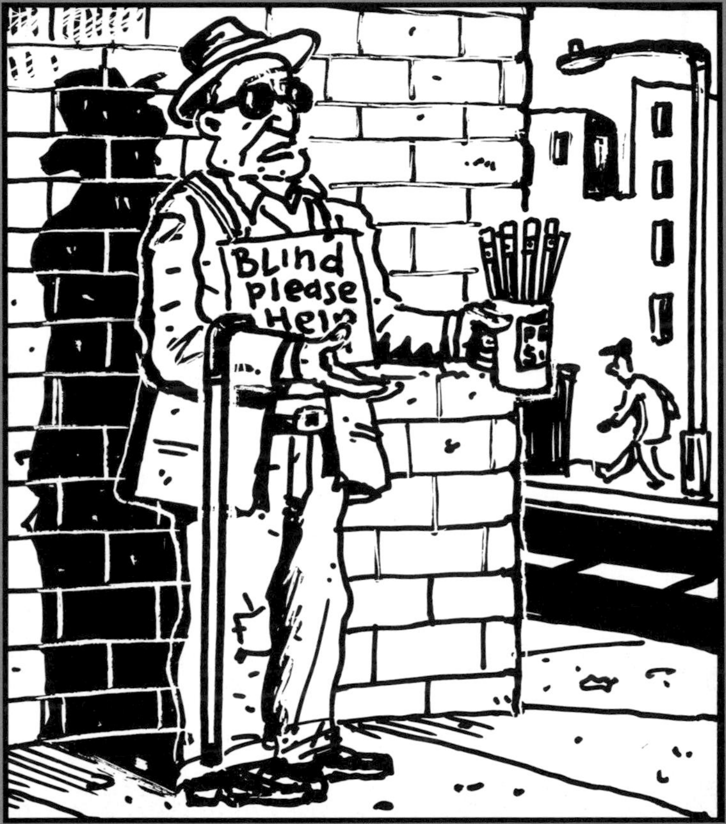
Blind please

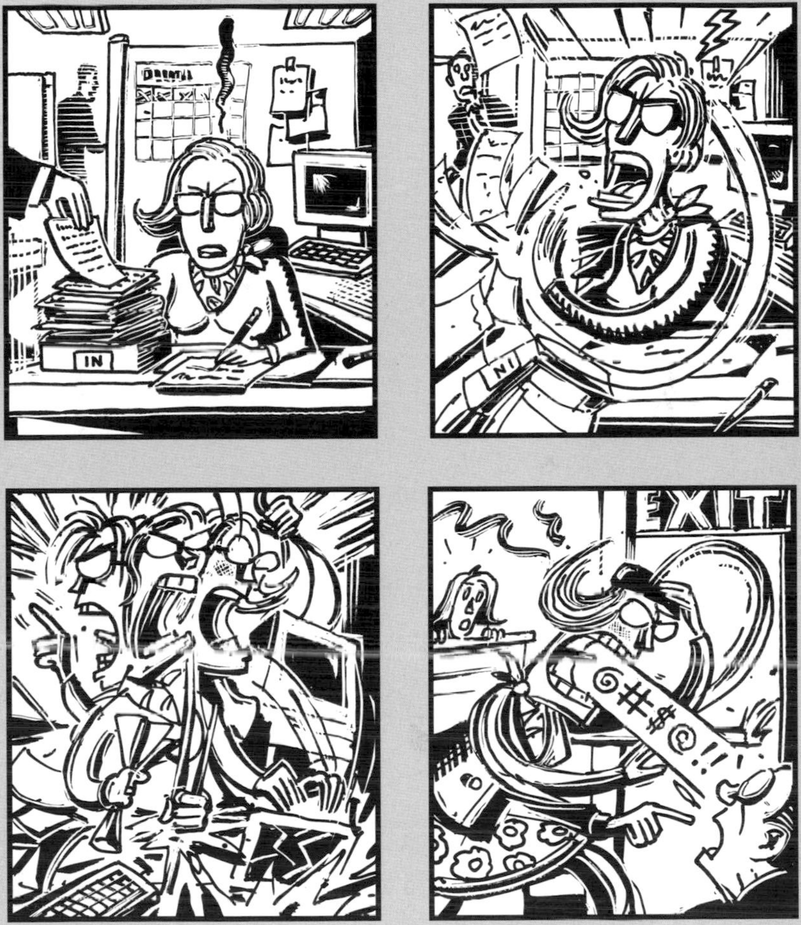
IN
NI
EXIT
@#$@!!

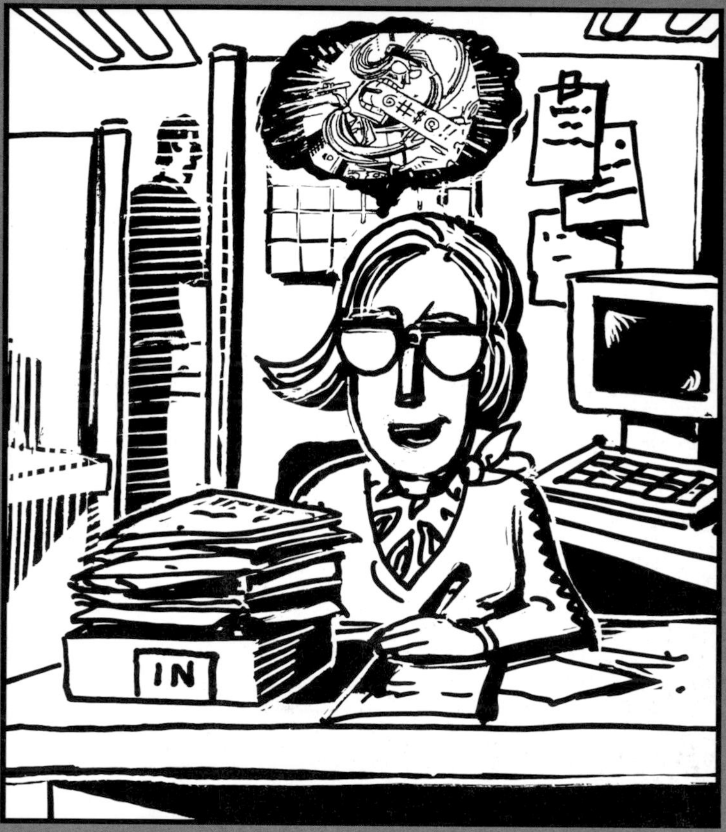
IN

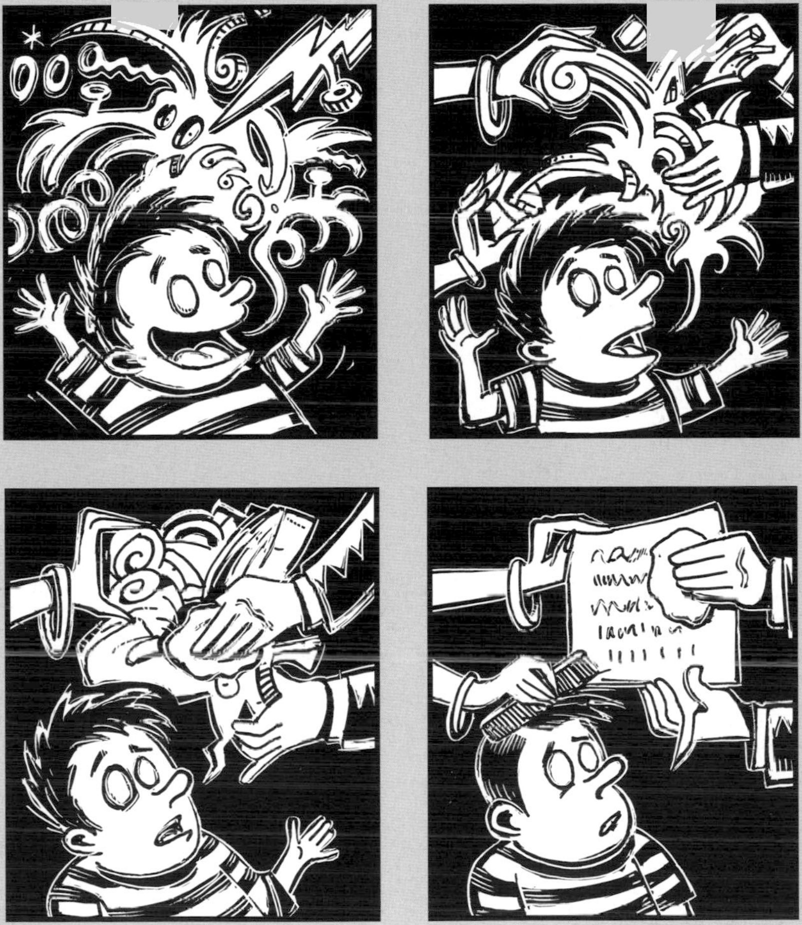

VOMEN

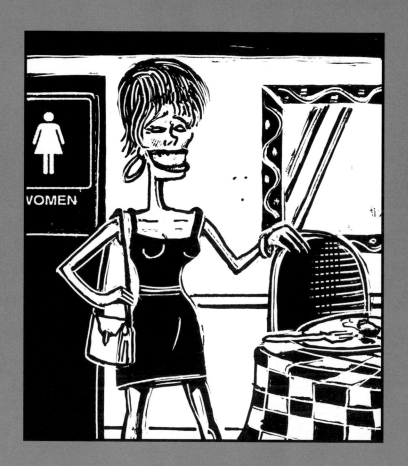

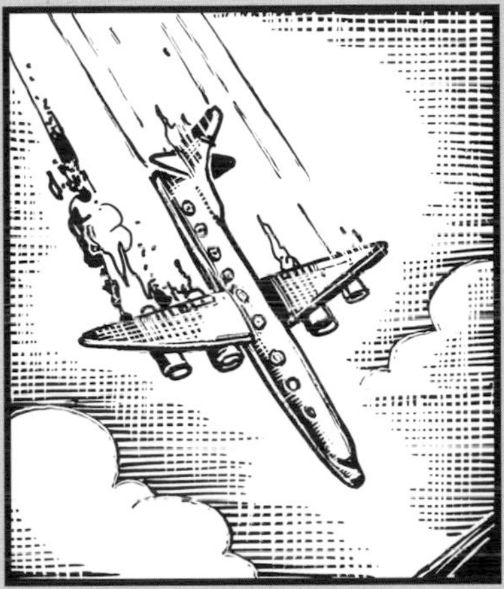

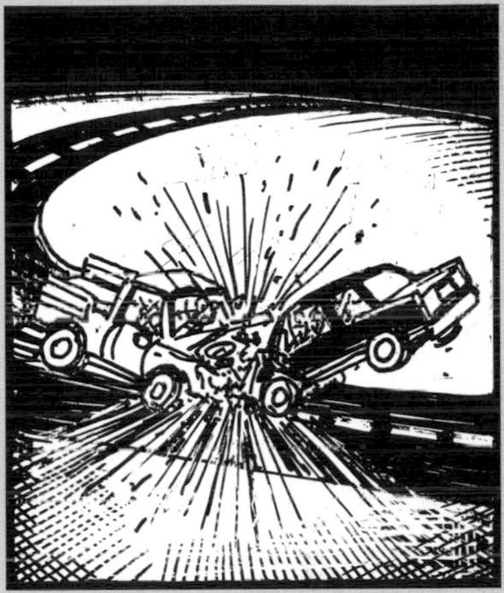

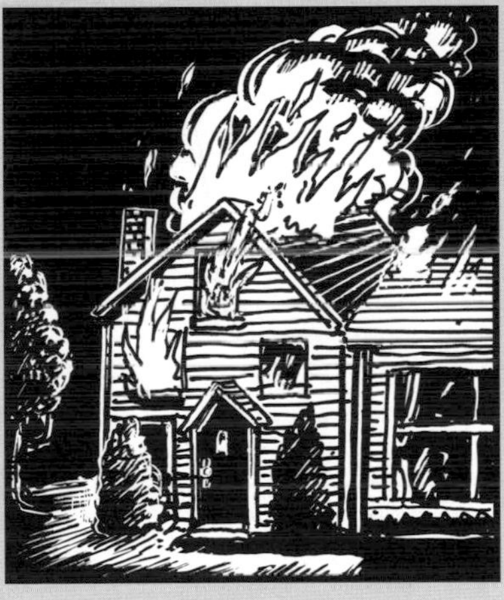

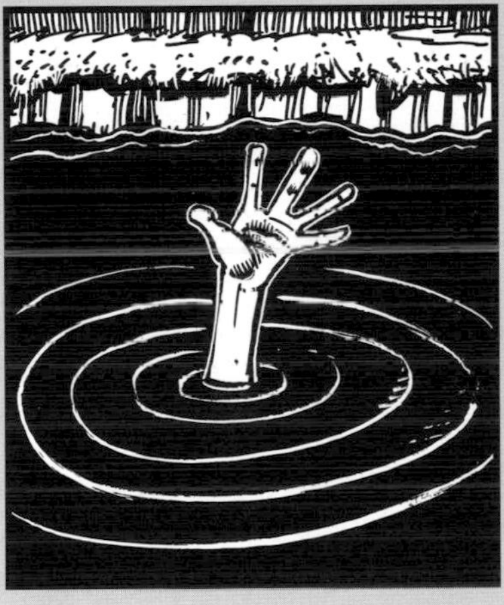

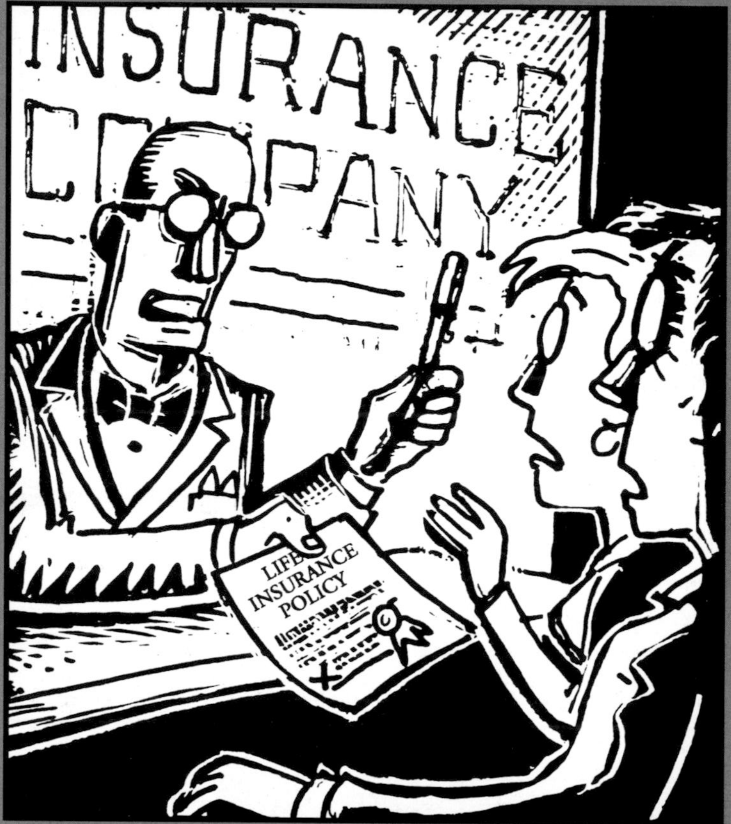
INSURANCE
LIFE
INSURANCE
POLICY

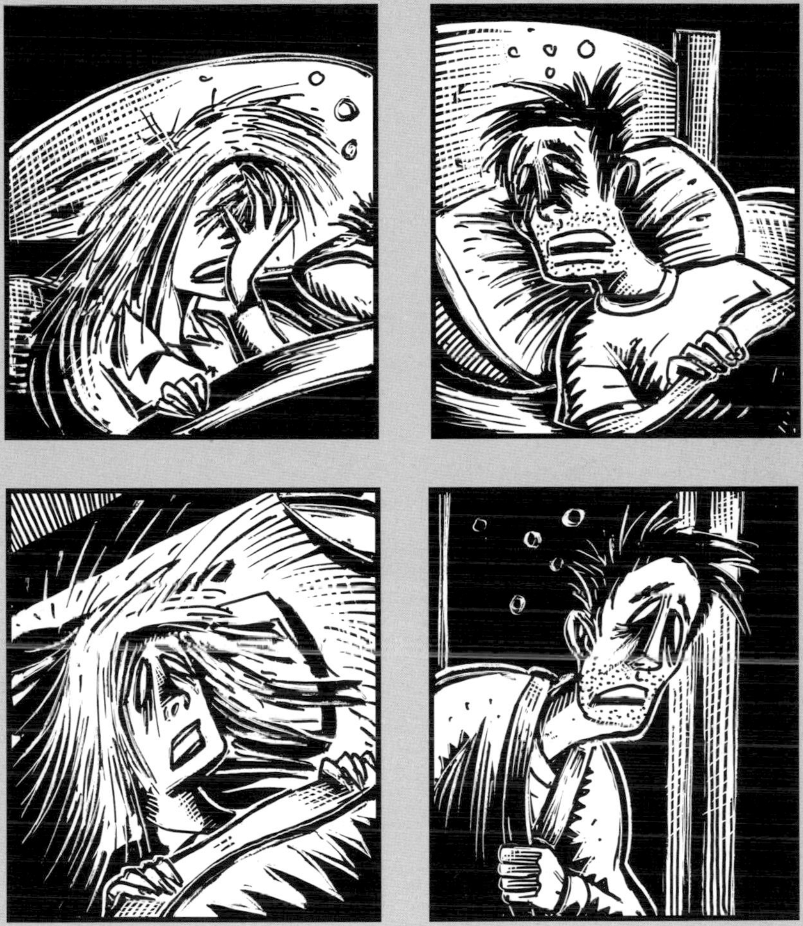

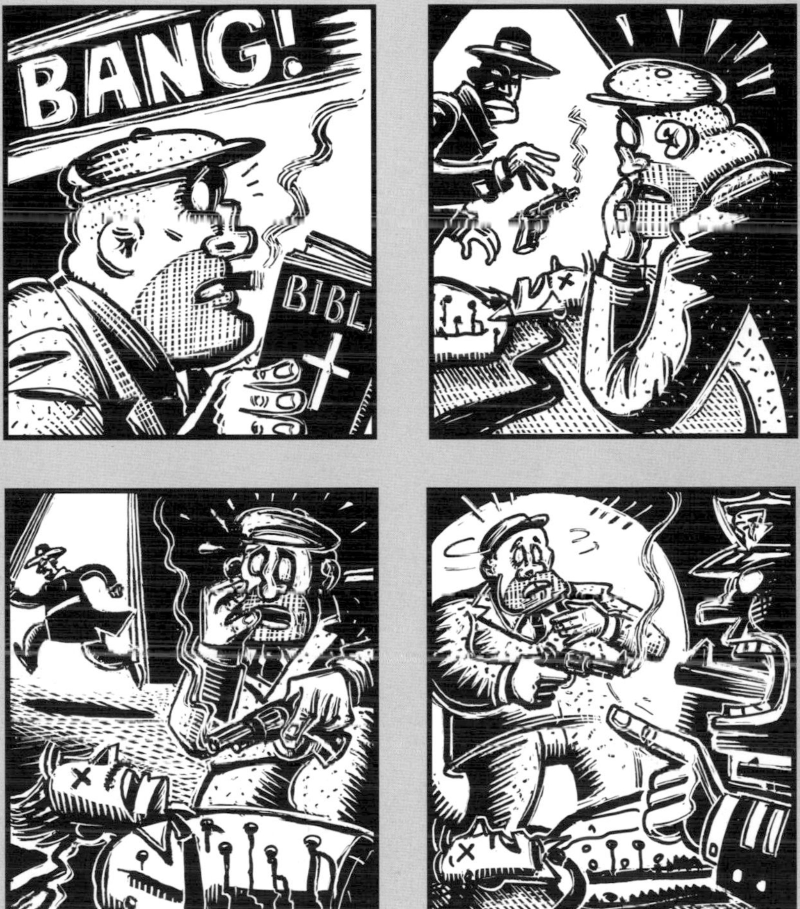
BANG!
BIBL

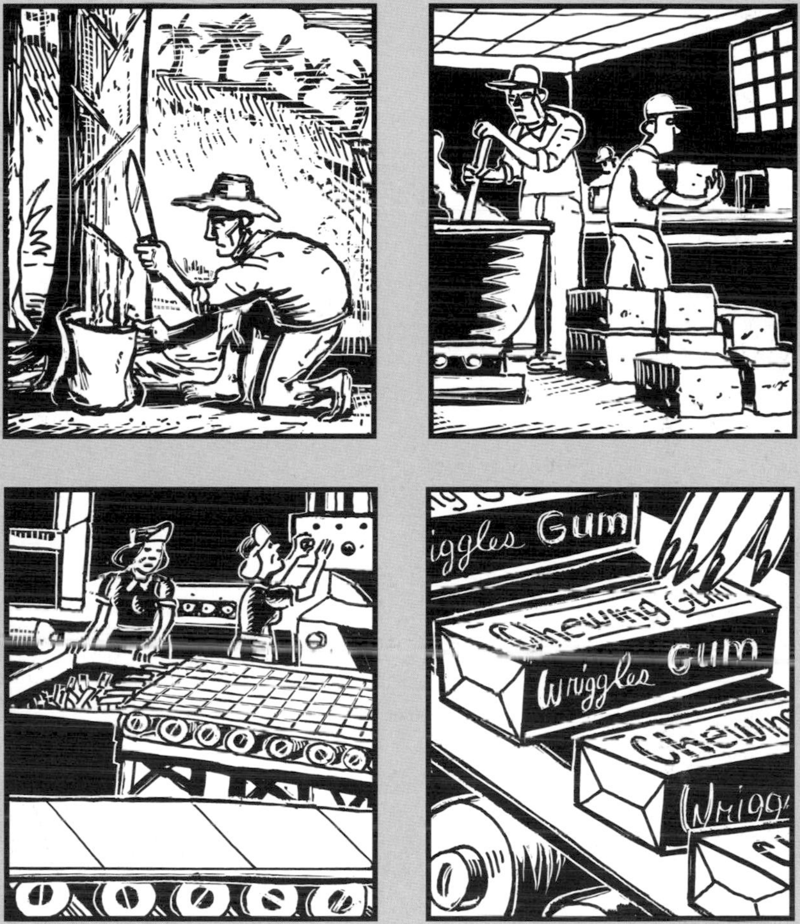
iggles Gum
Chewing Gum
Wriggles Gum

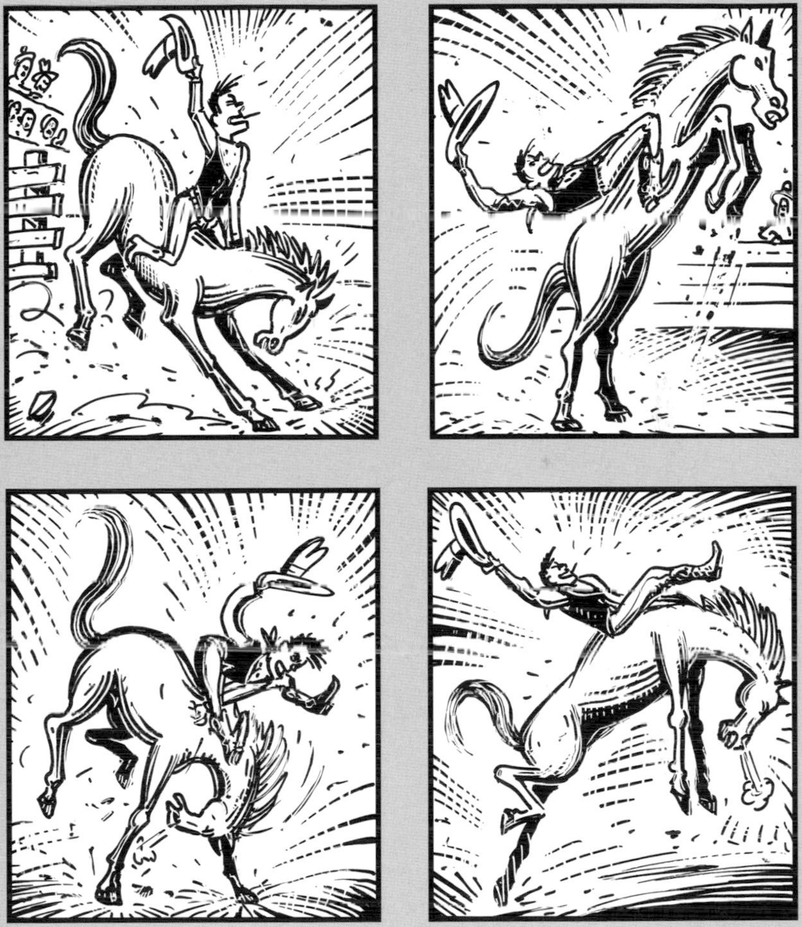

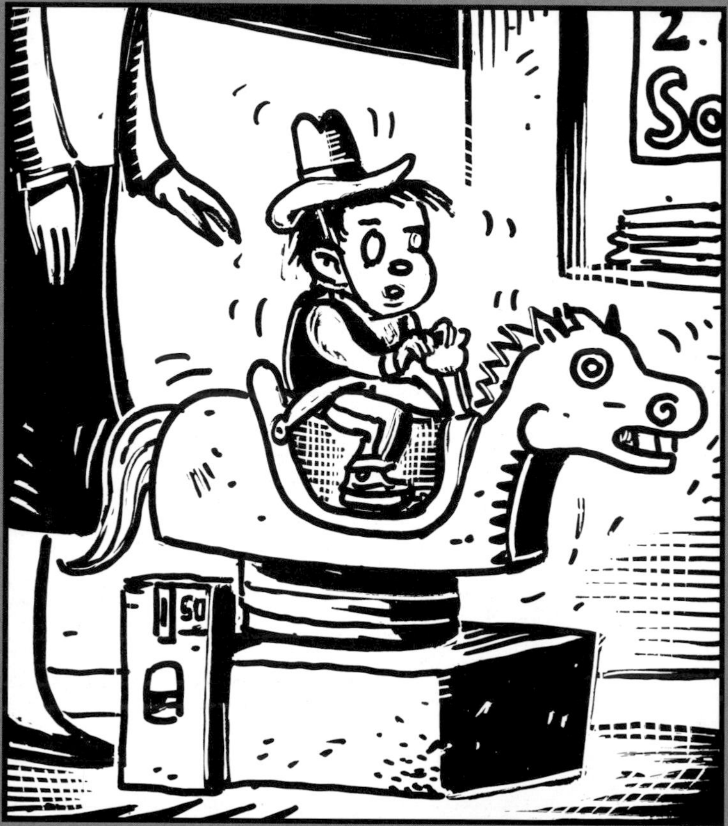
2.
So
50

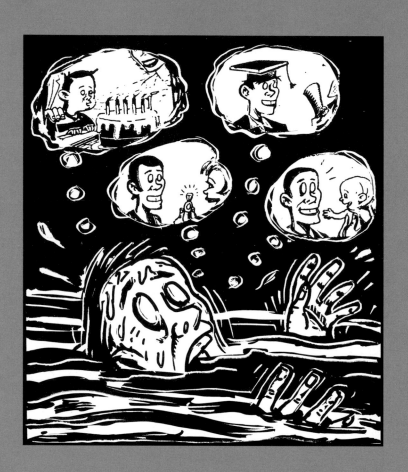

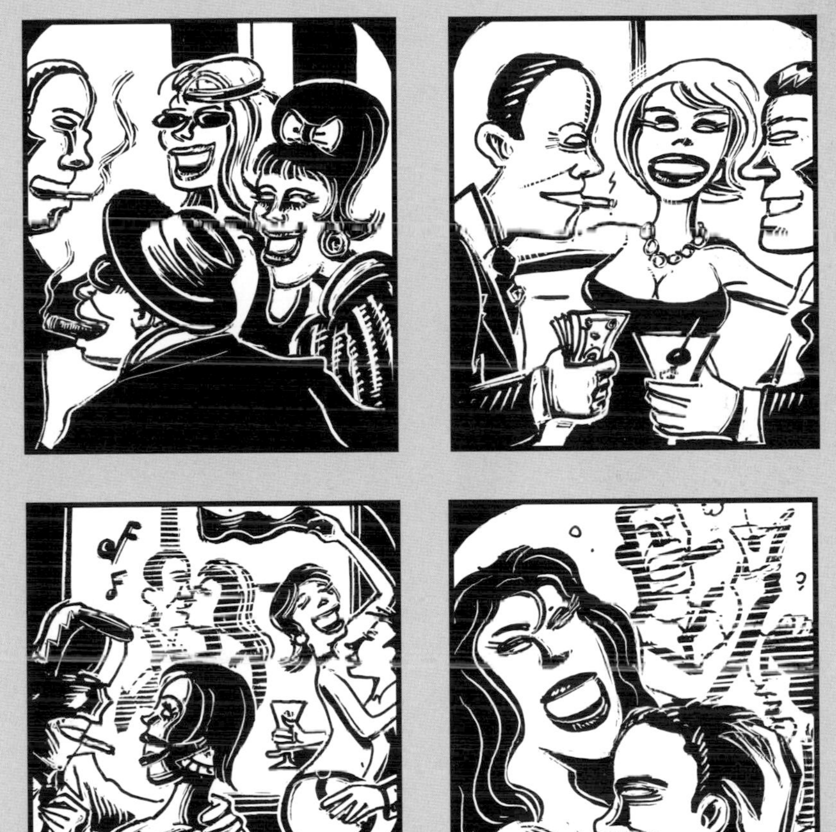

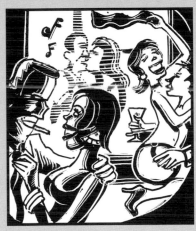

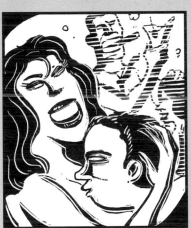

FBI

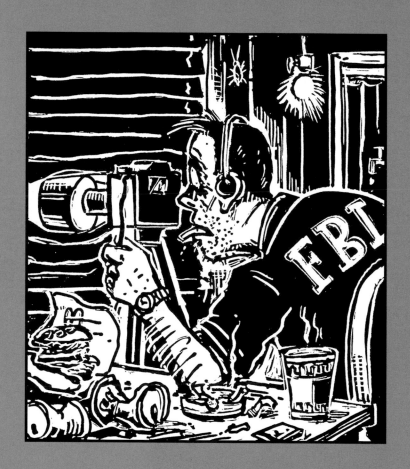

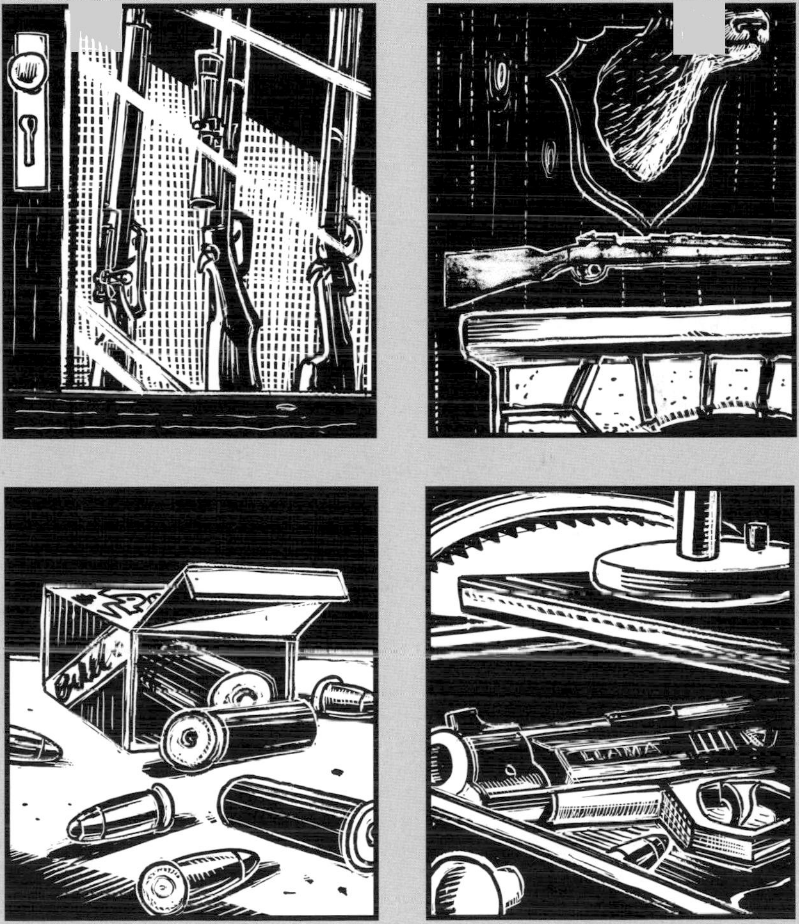
LLAMA

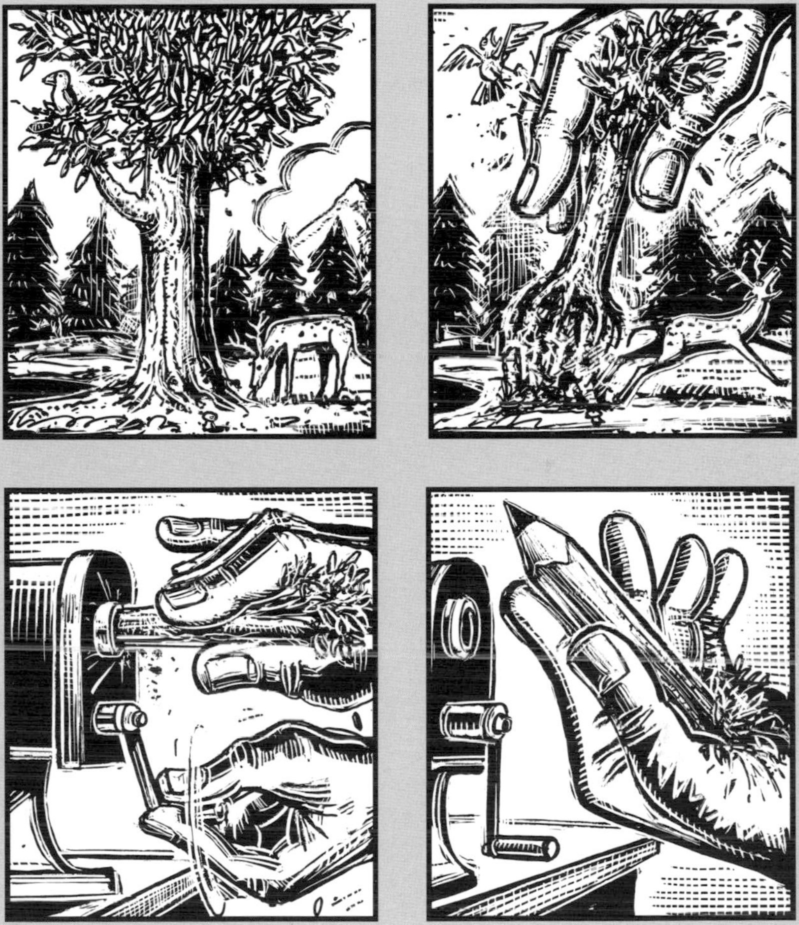

1-86
210
17798186
DATE
PETER KUPER,
NEW YORK, NY 10025-5440
SAVE THE TREES FUND
MEMO
CHARITY

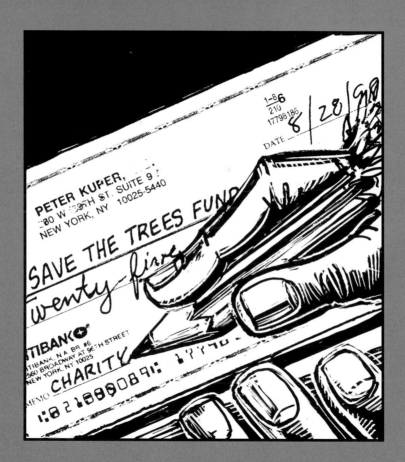

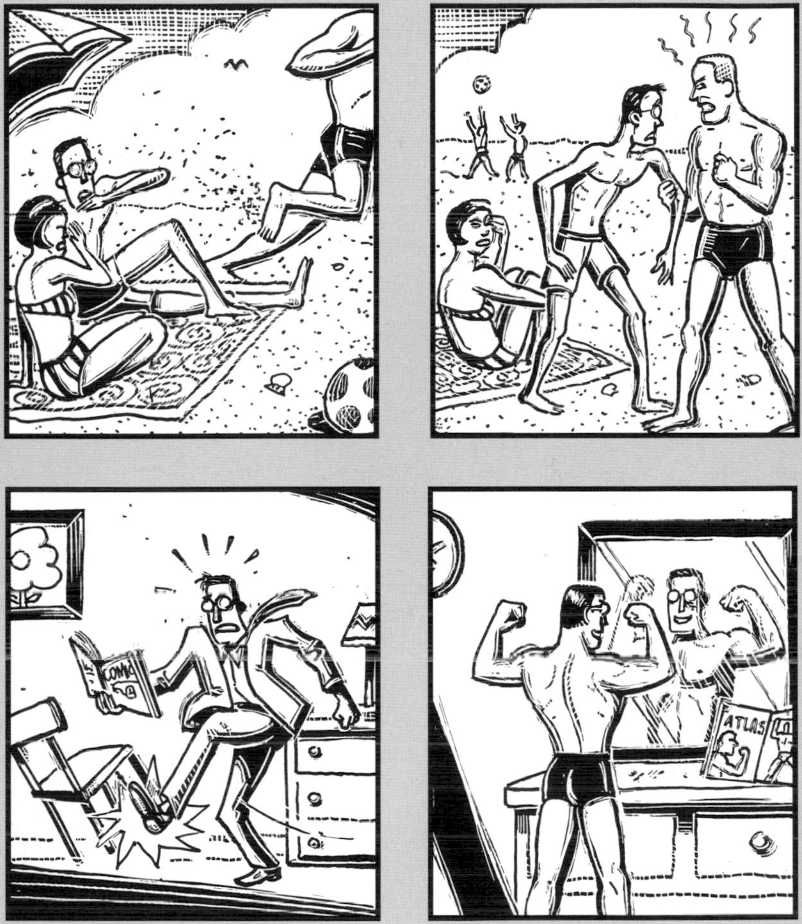
COMIC
ATLAS

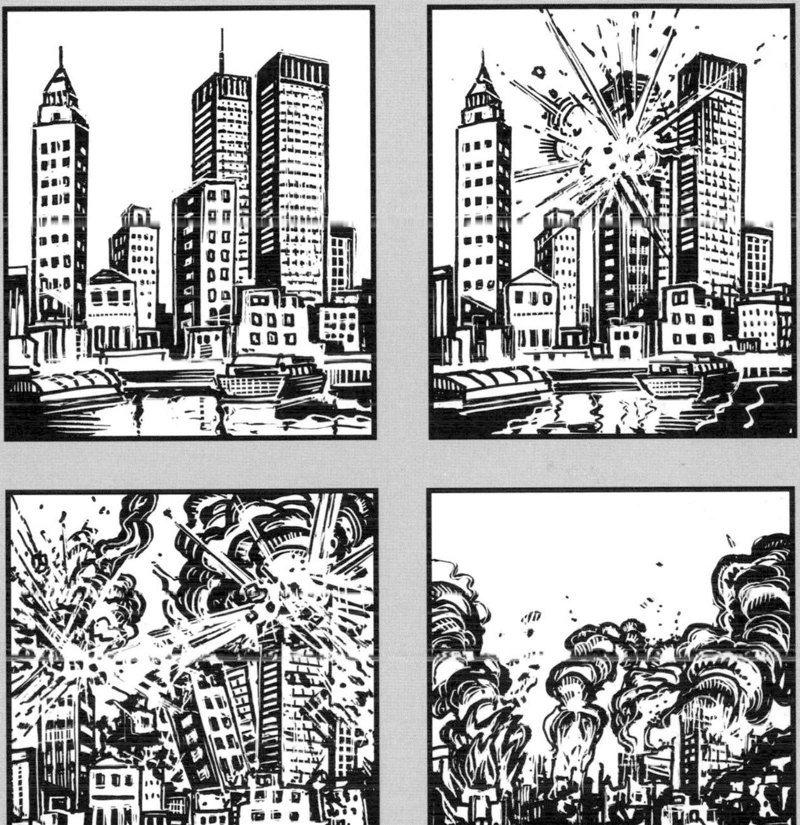

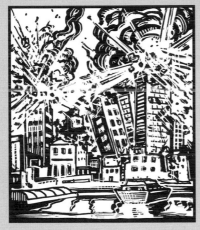

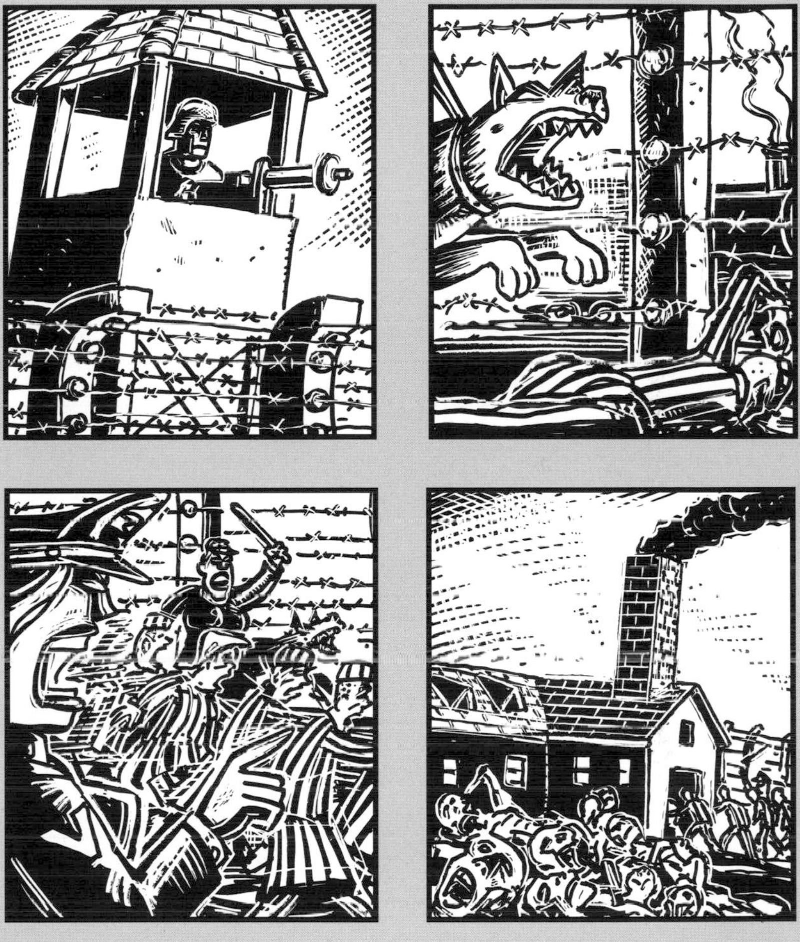

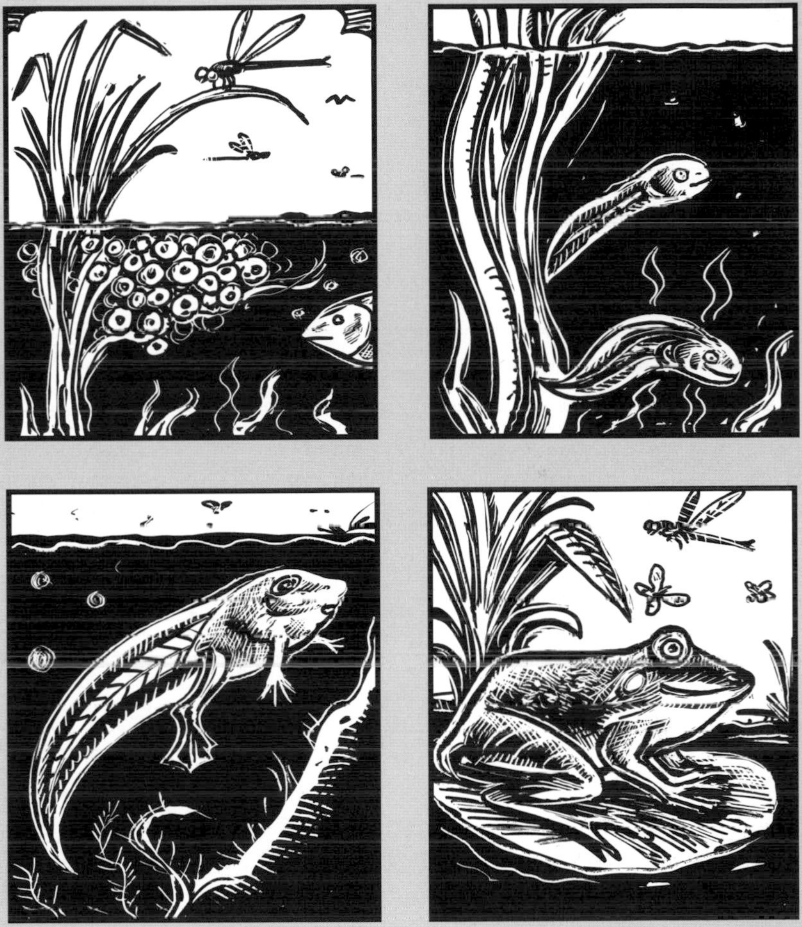

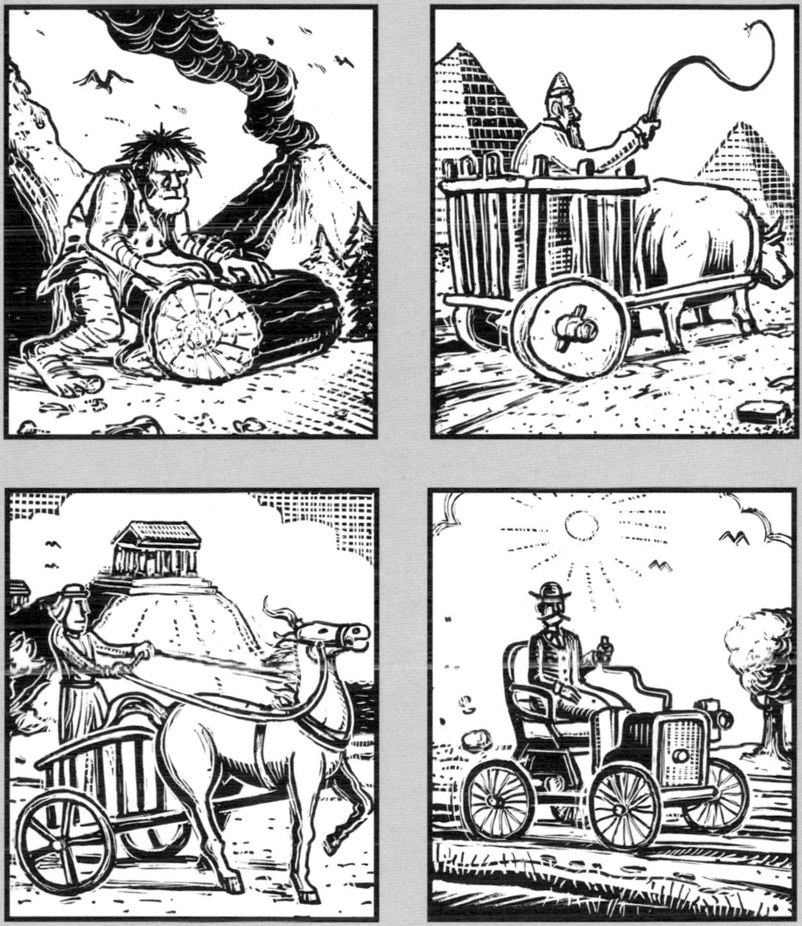

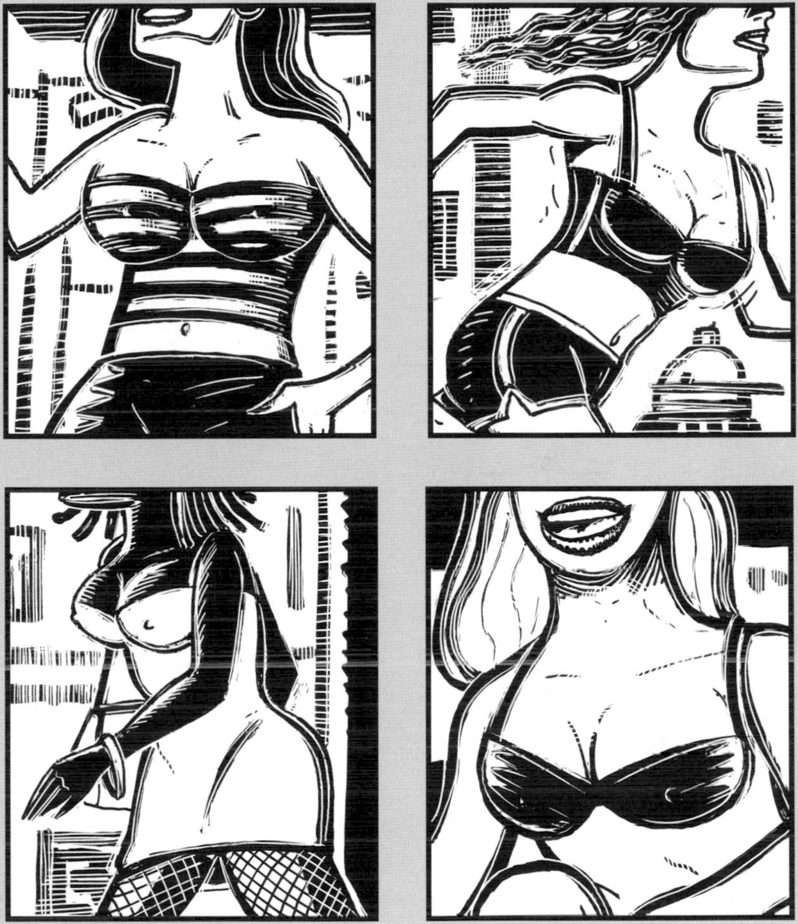

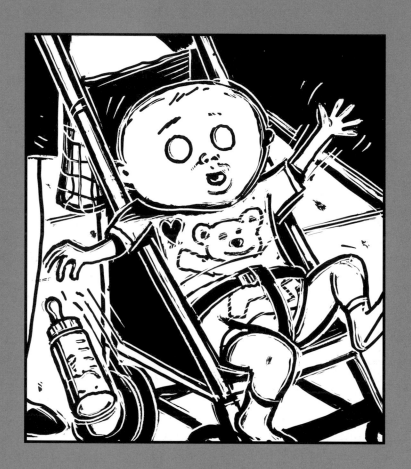

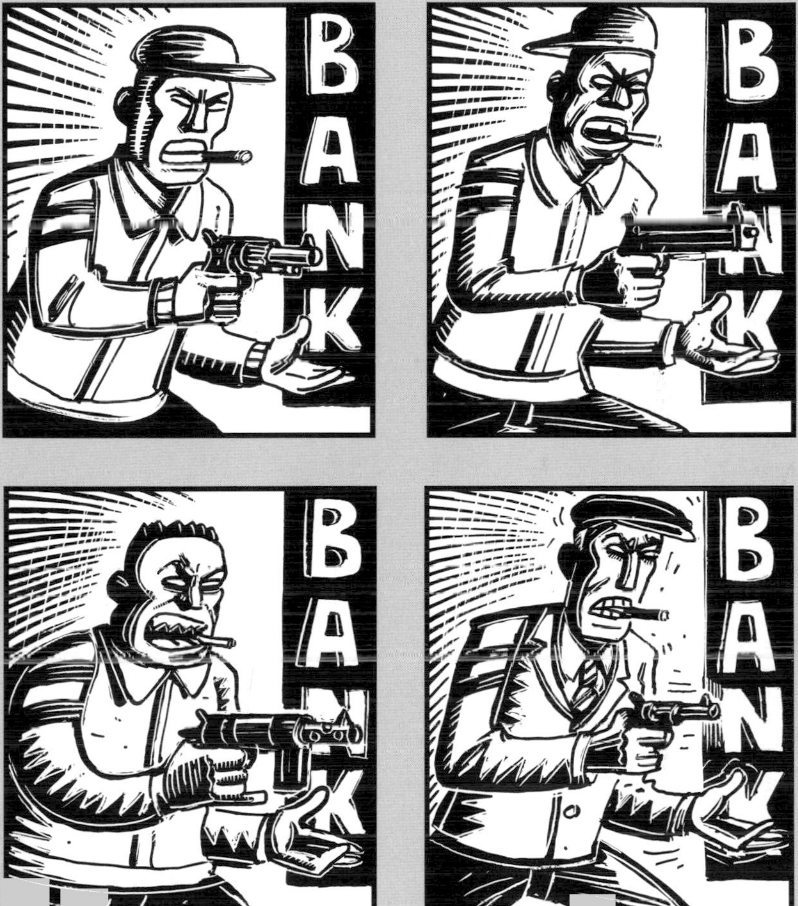
BANK
BANK
BANK
BAN

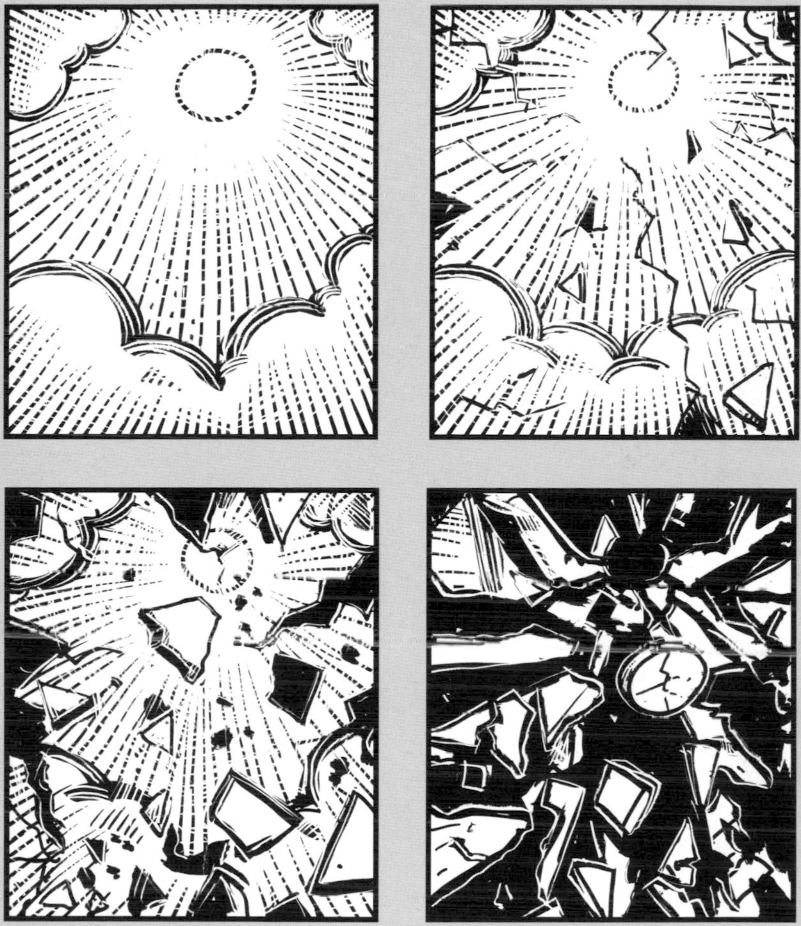

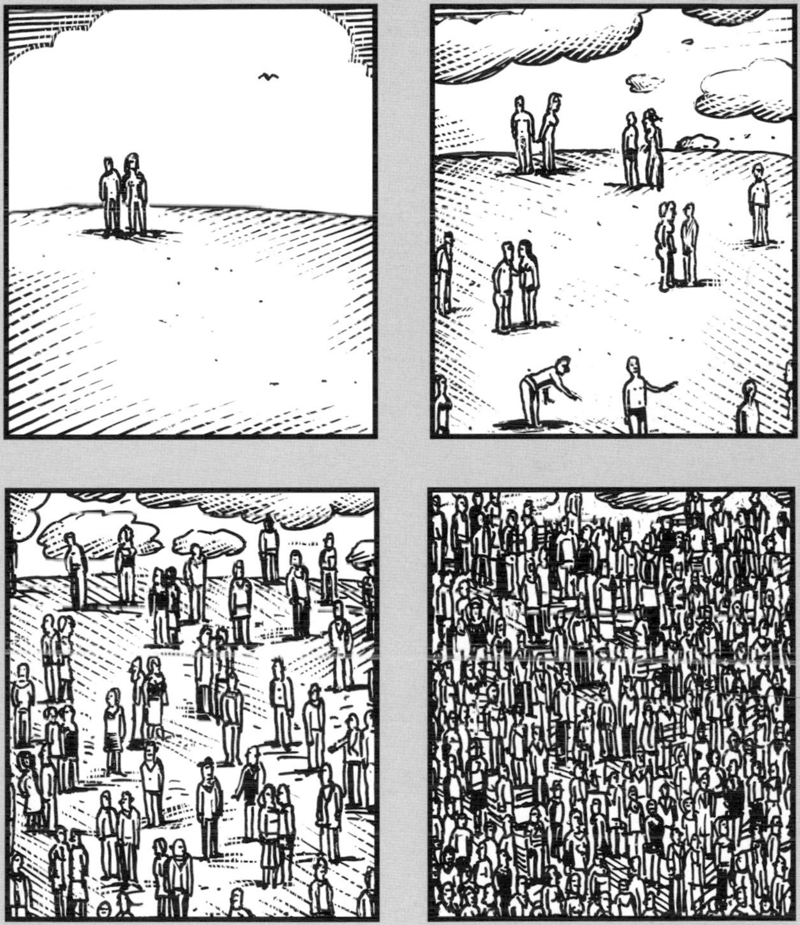

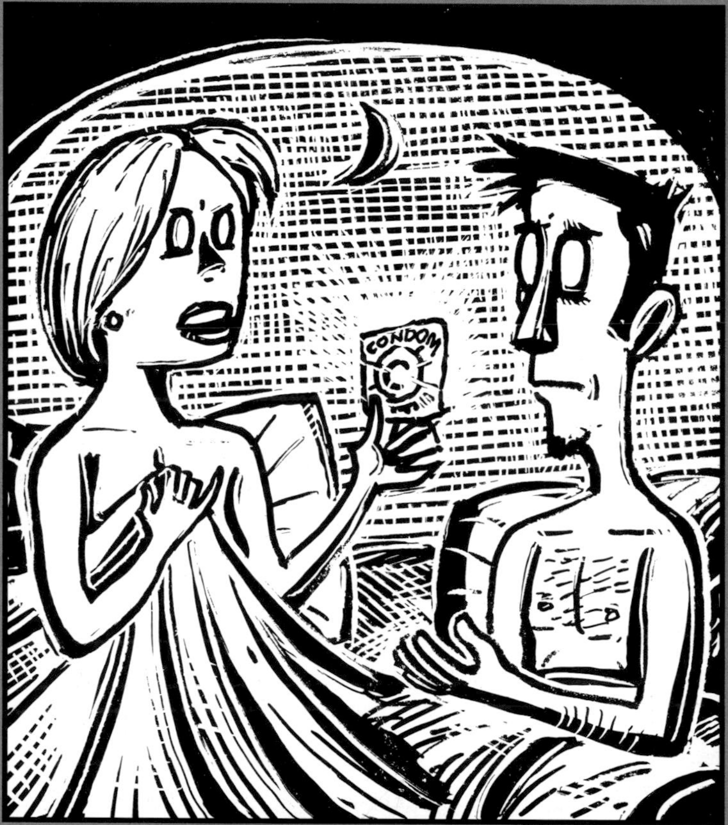
CONDOM

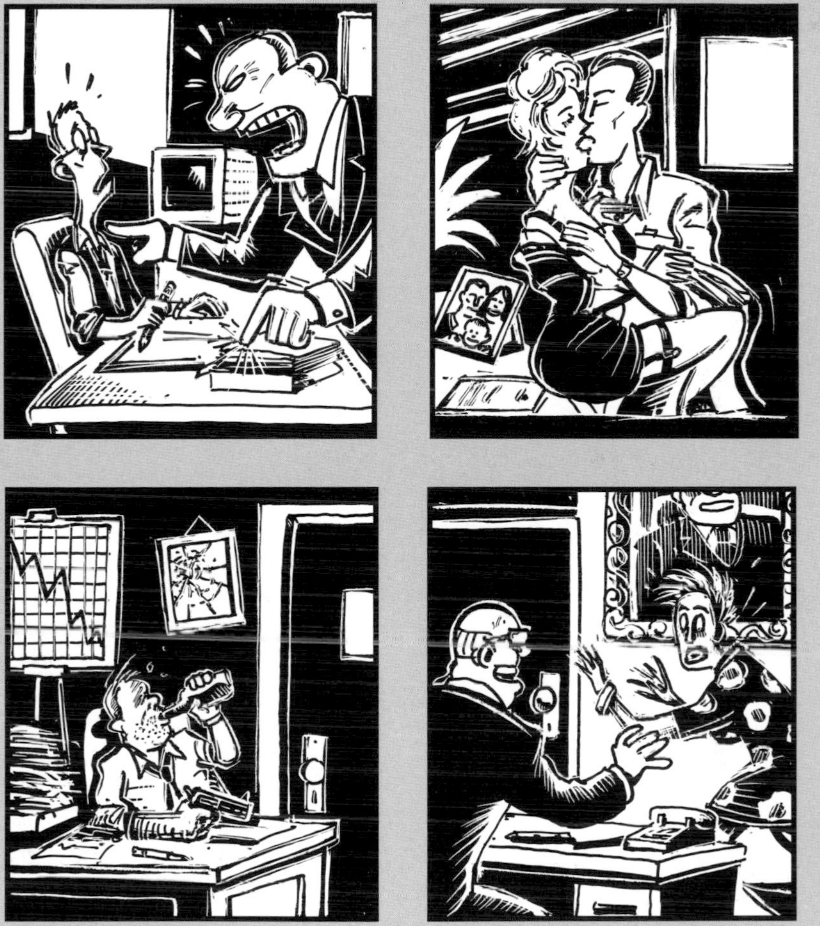

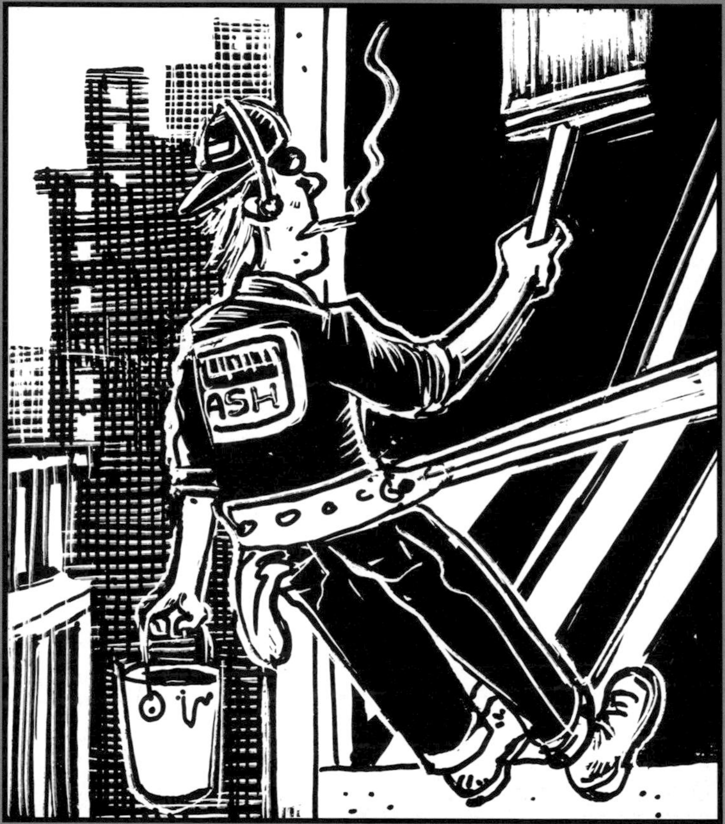
ASH

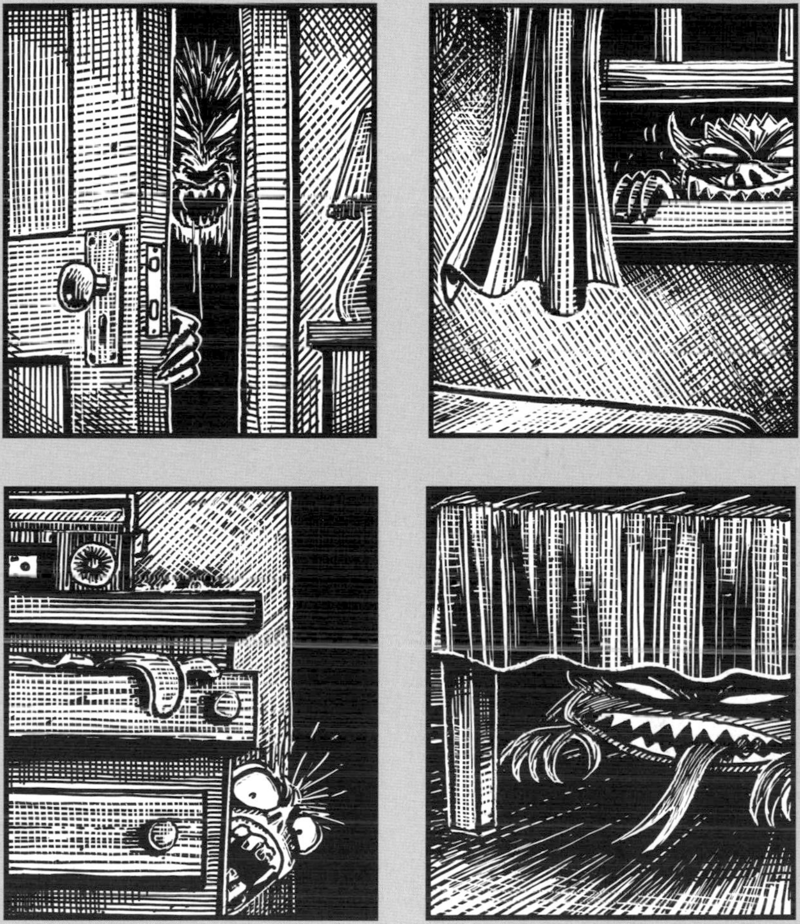

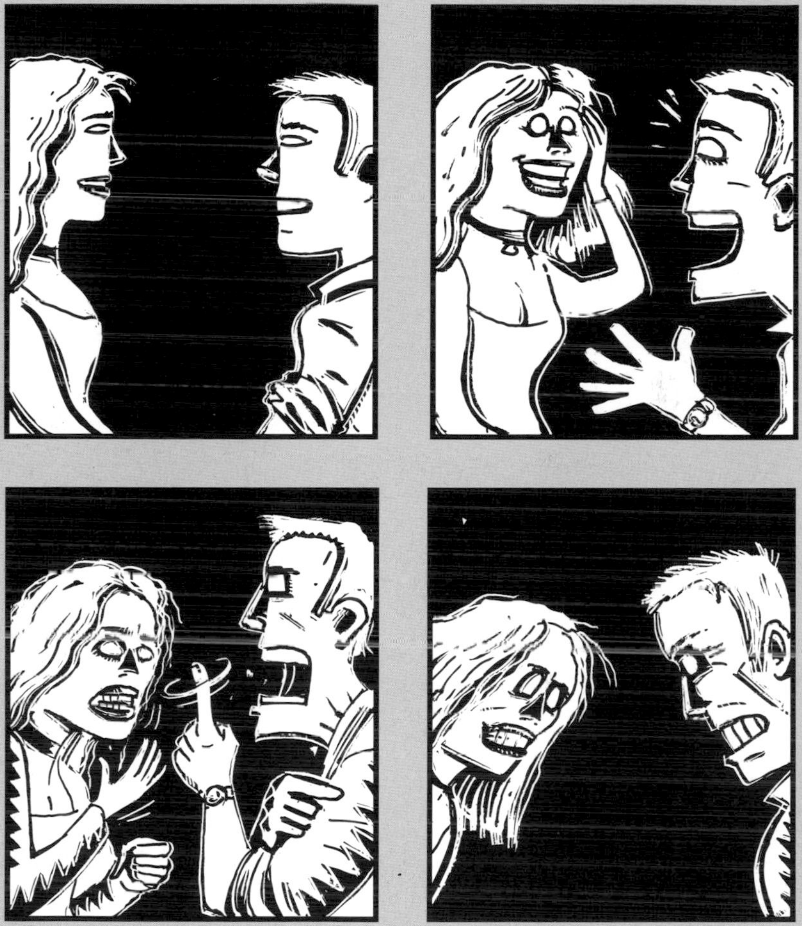

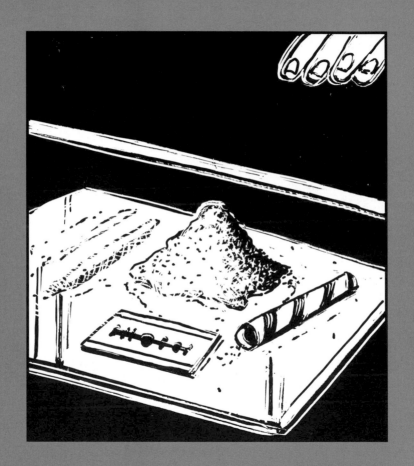

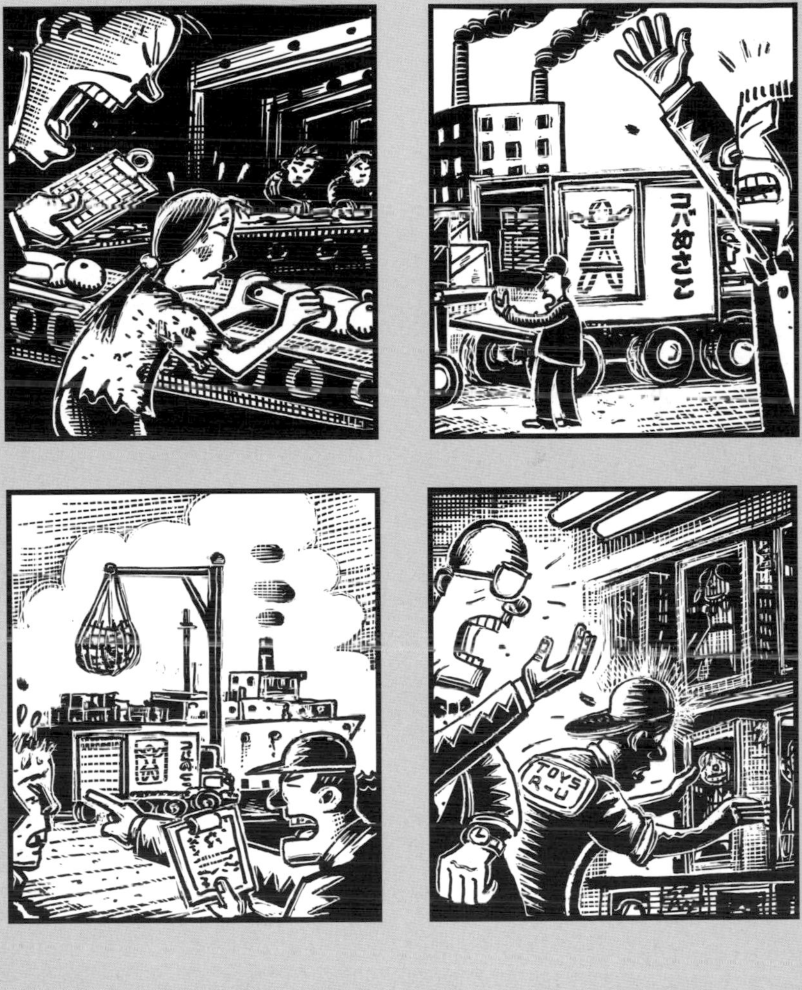
TOYS
R-U

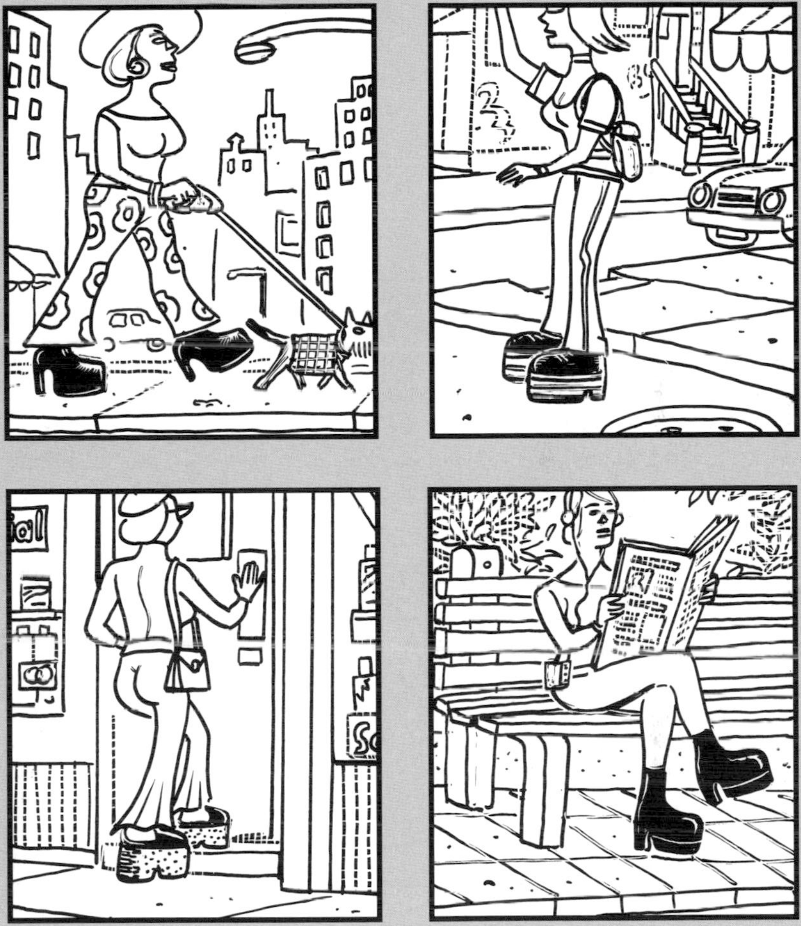

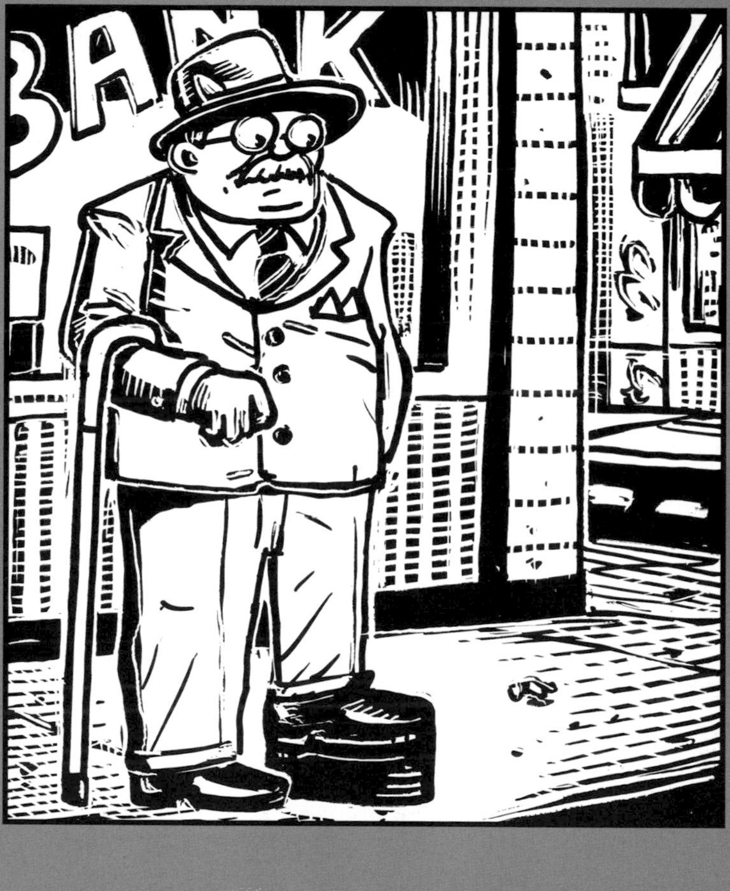
BANK

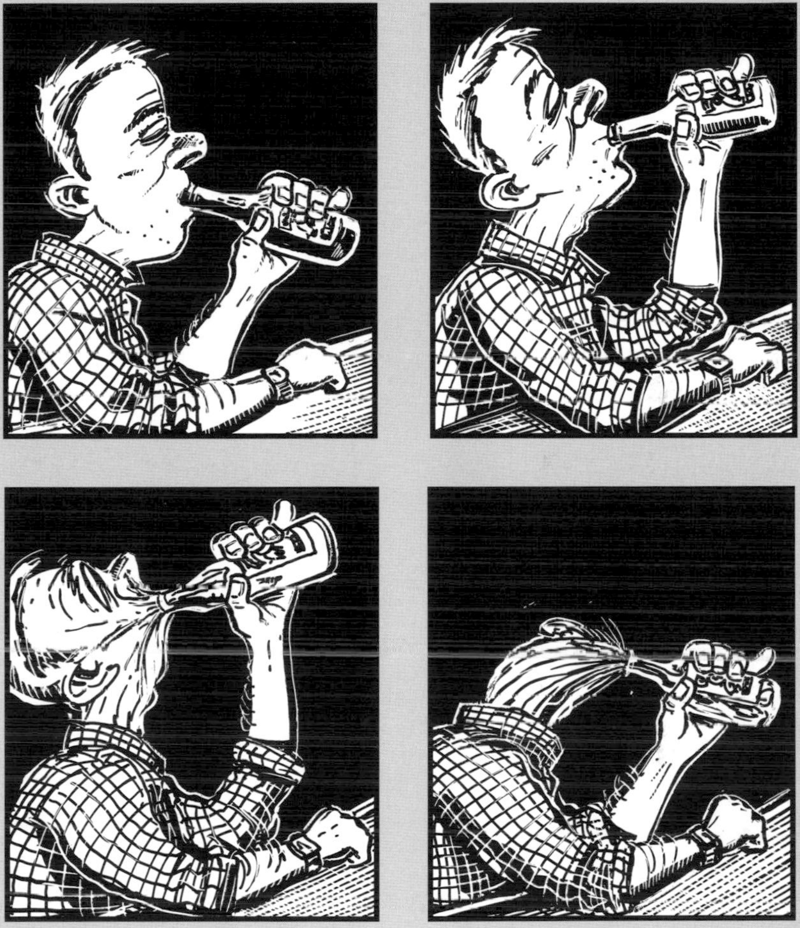

VALDEZ
POISON
FRITO

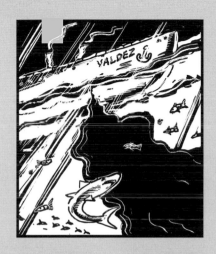

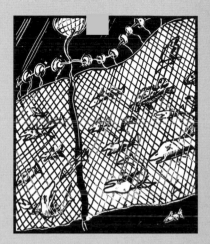

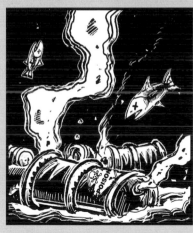

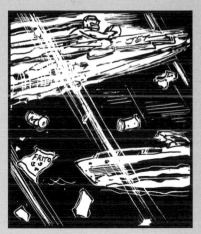

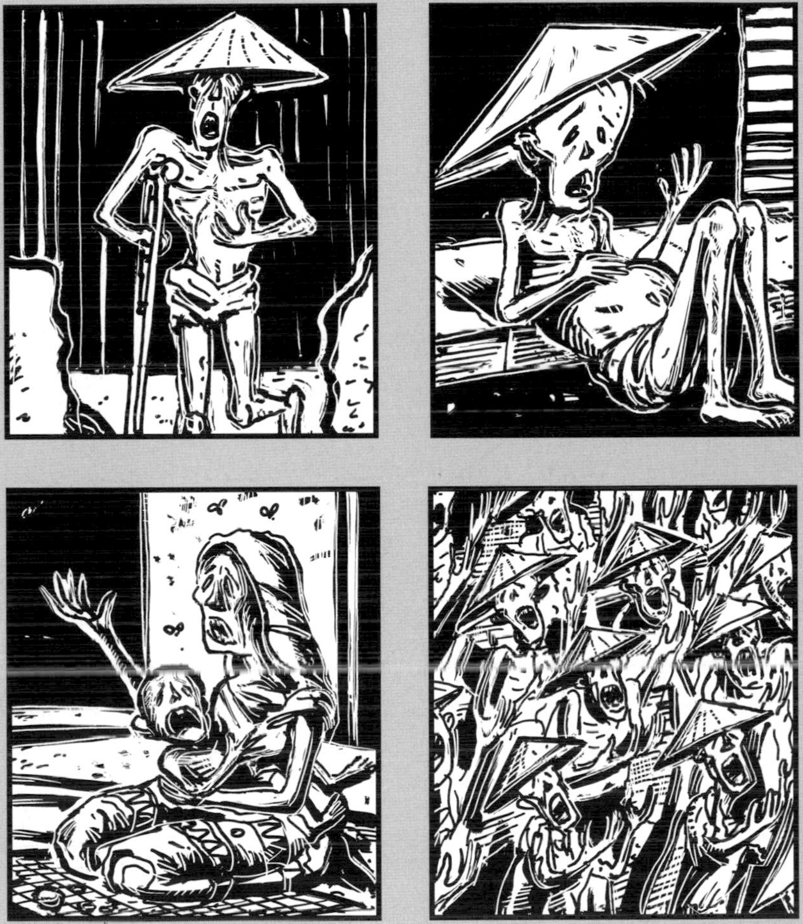

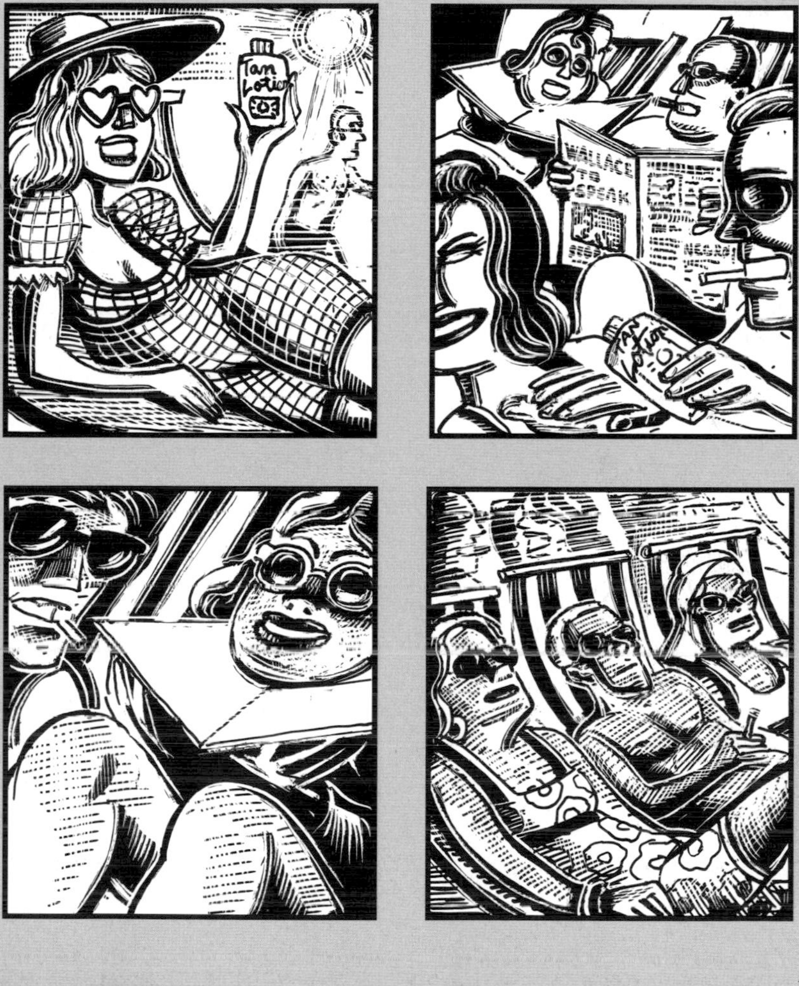
Tan Lotion
WALLACE TO SPEAK
NEGRO

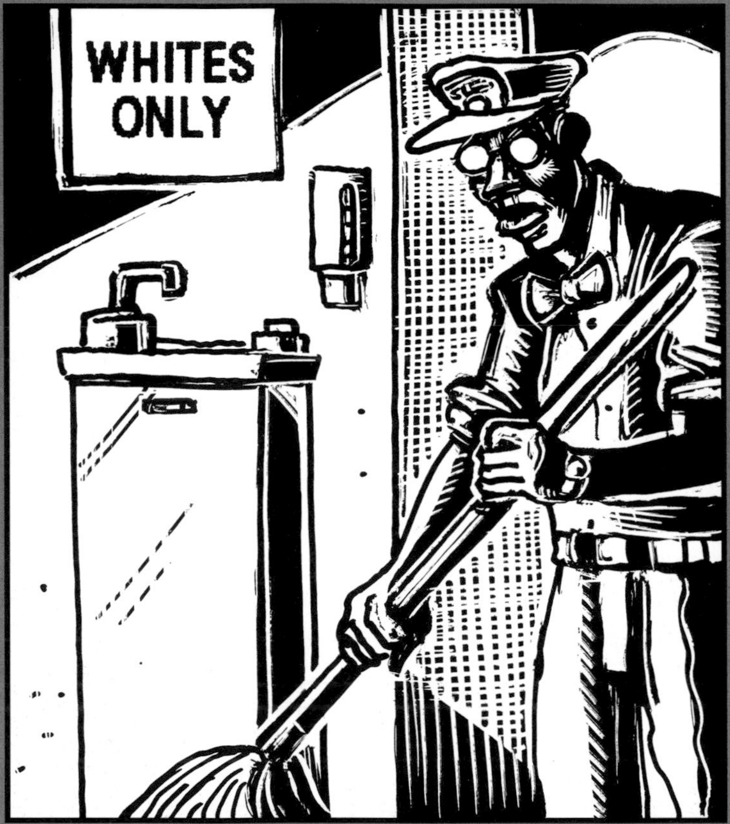
WHITES
ONLY

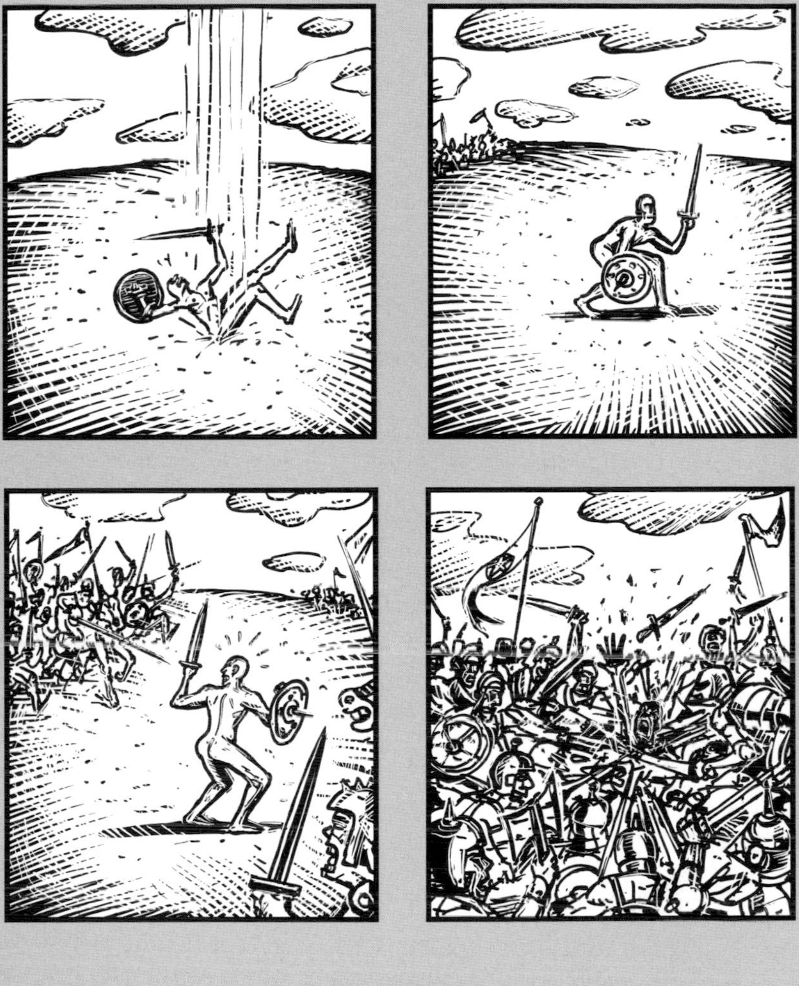

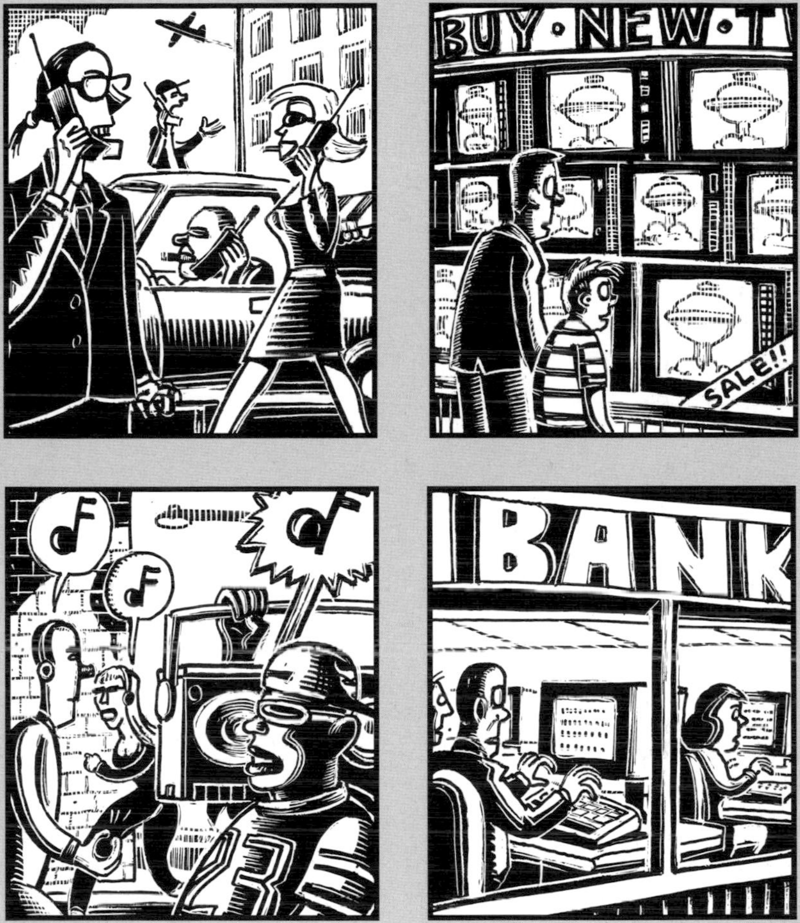
BUY•NEW•T
SALE!!
BANK

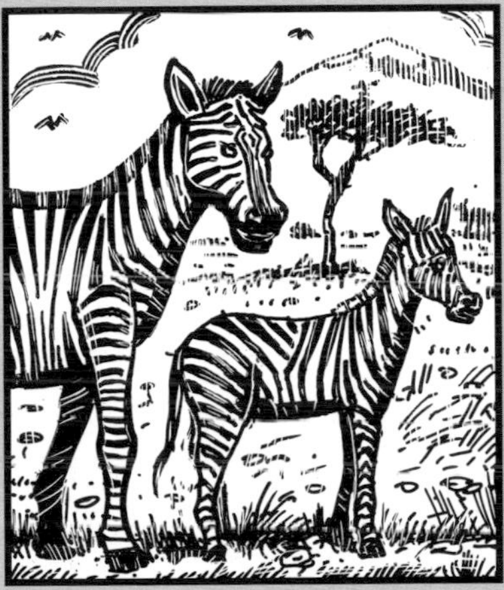

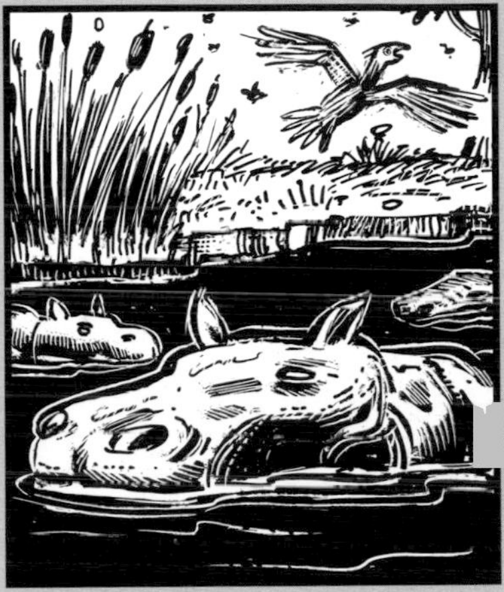

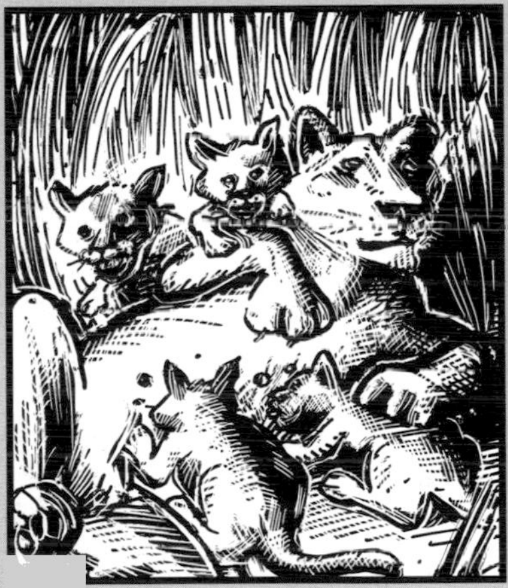

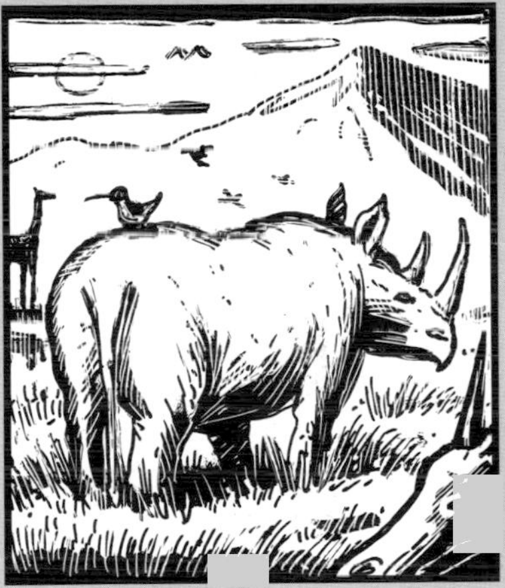

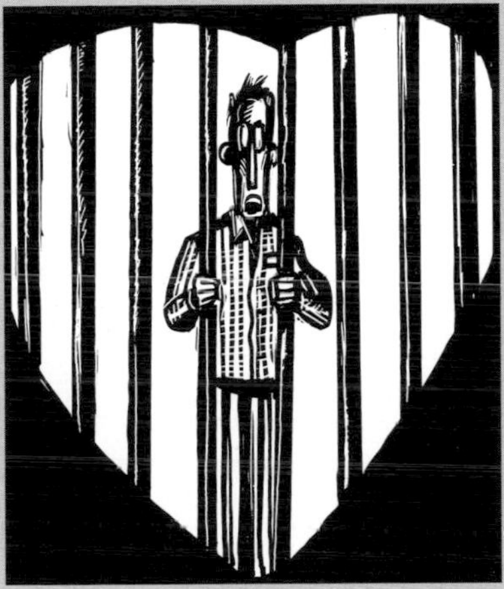

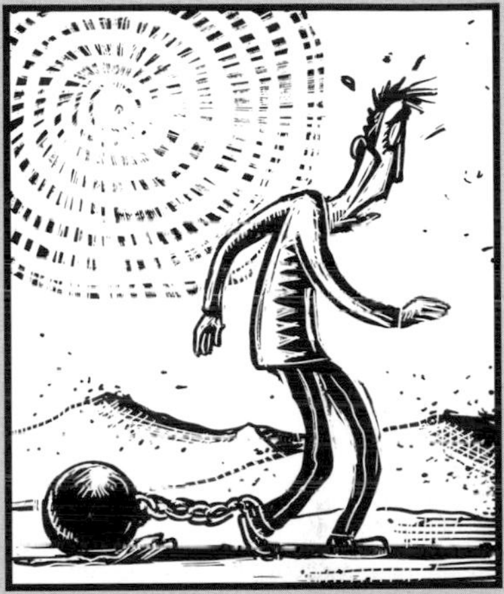

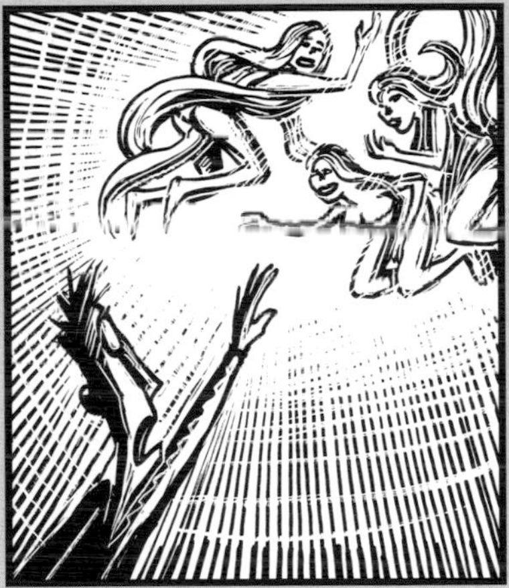

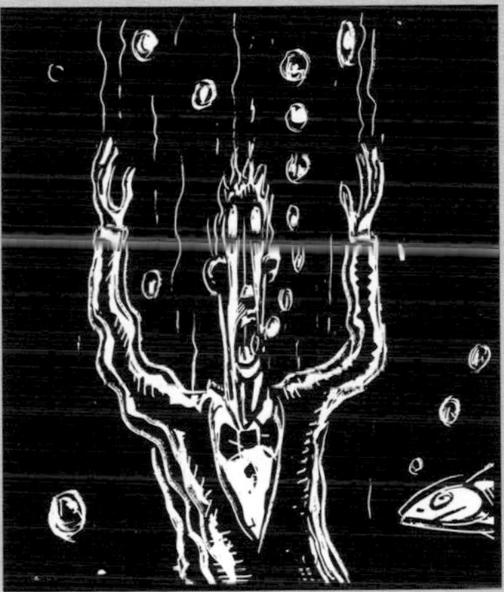

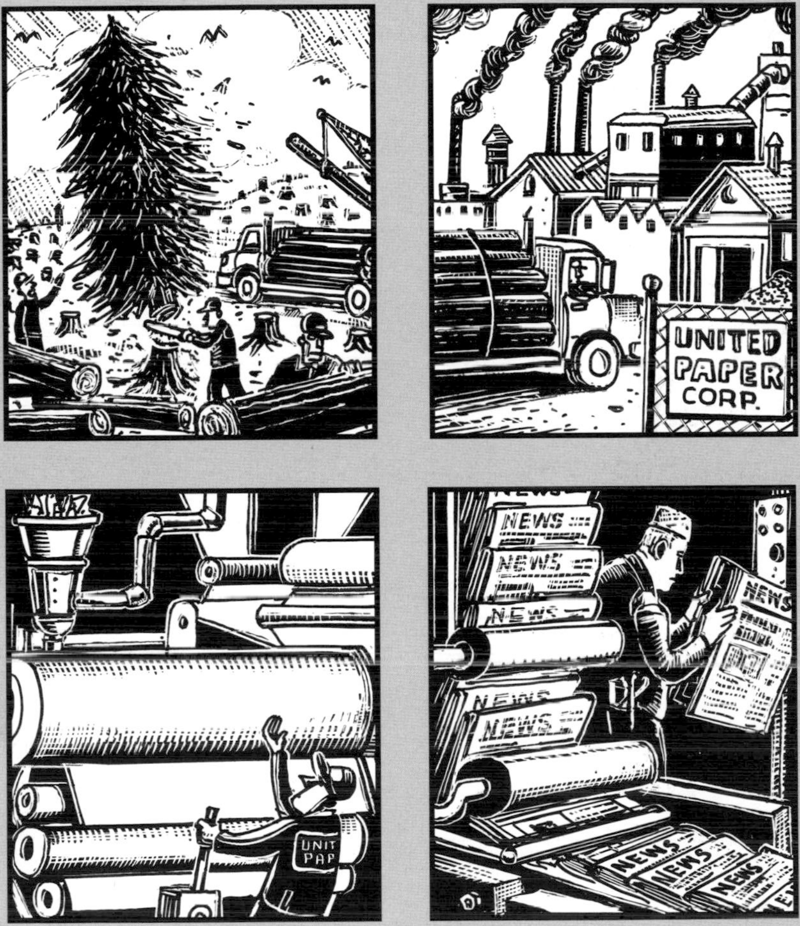
UNITED
PAPER
CORP.
UNIT
PAP
NEWS
NEWS
NEWS
NEWS
NEWS
NEWS
NEWS
NEWS
NEWS

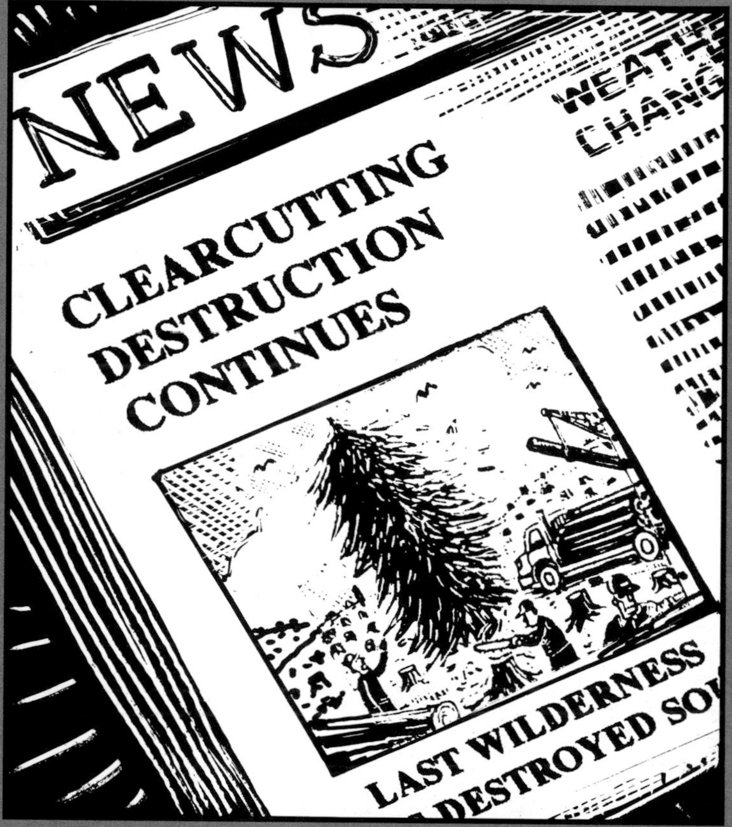

NEWS
CLEARCUTTING DESTRUCTION CONTINUES
LAST WILDERNESS
DESTROYED SO

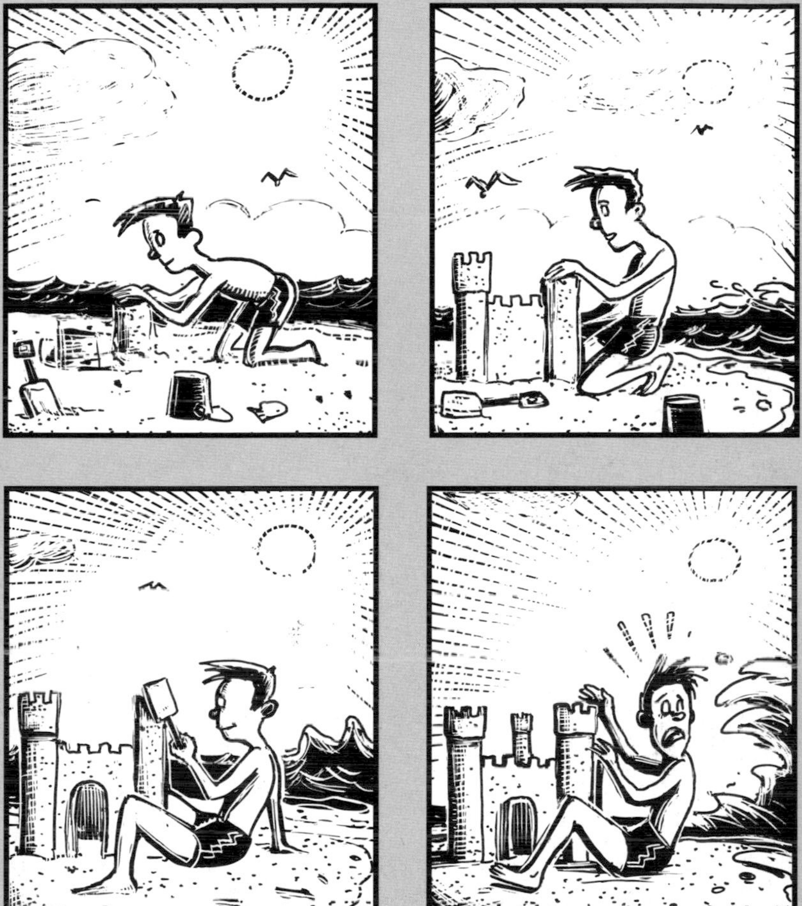

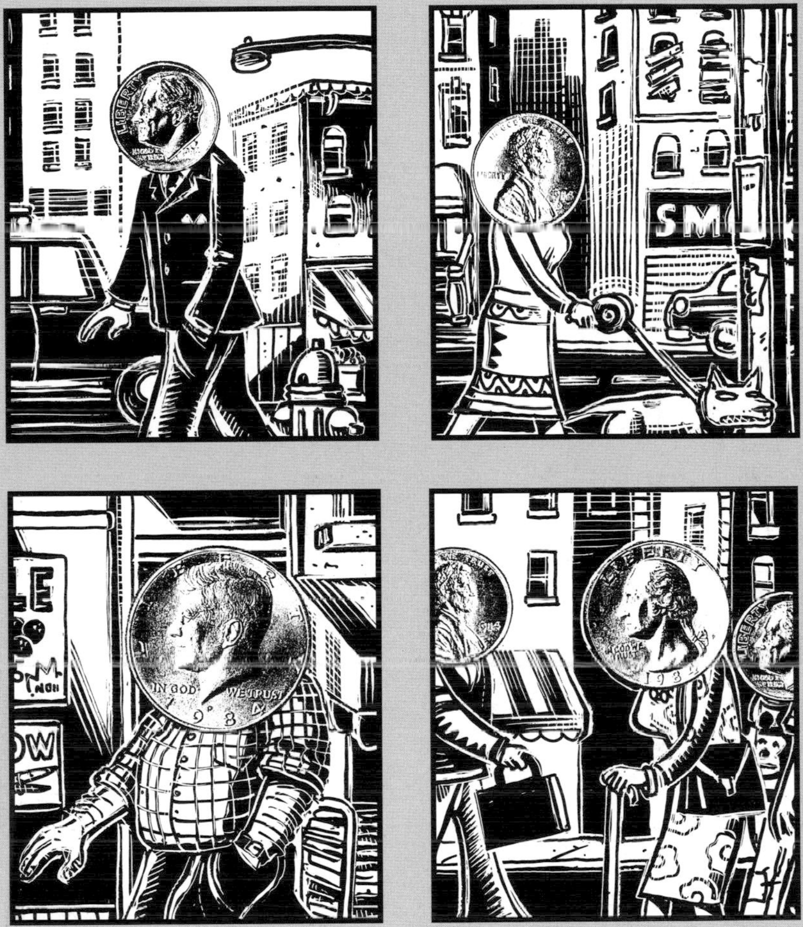
LIBERTY
SM
LE
OW
IN GOD WE TRUST
1984
LIBERTY

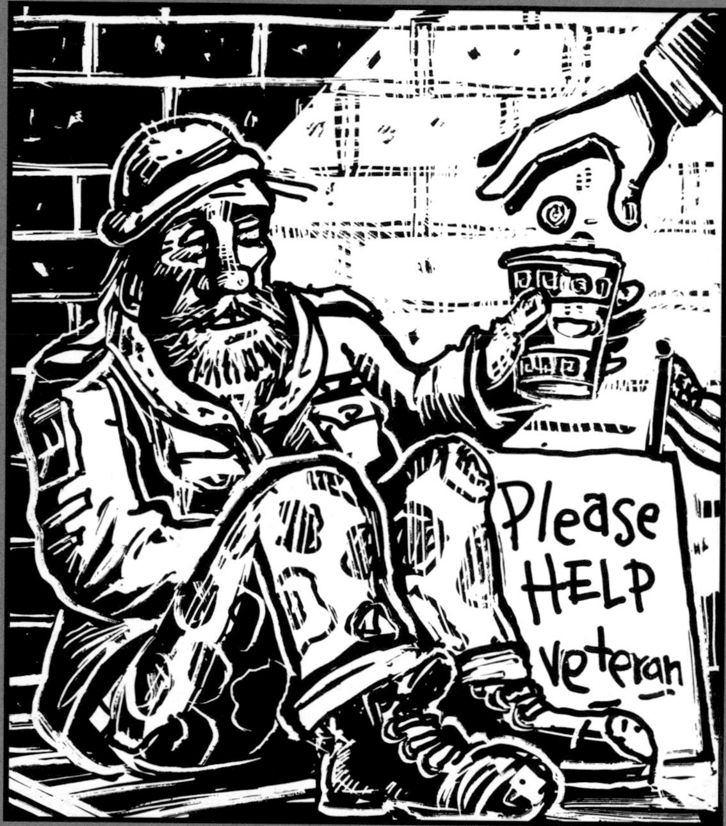
Please
HELP
veteran

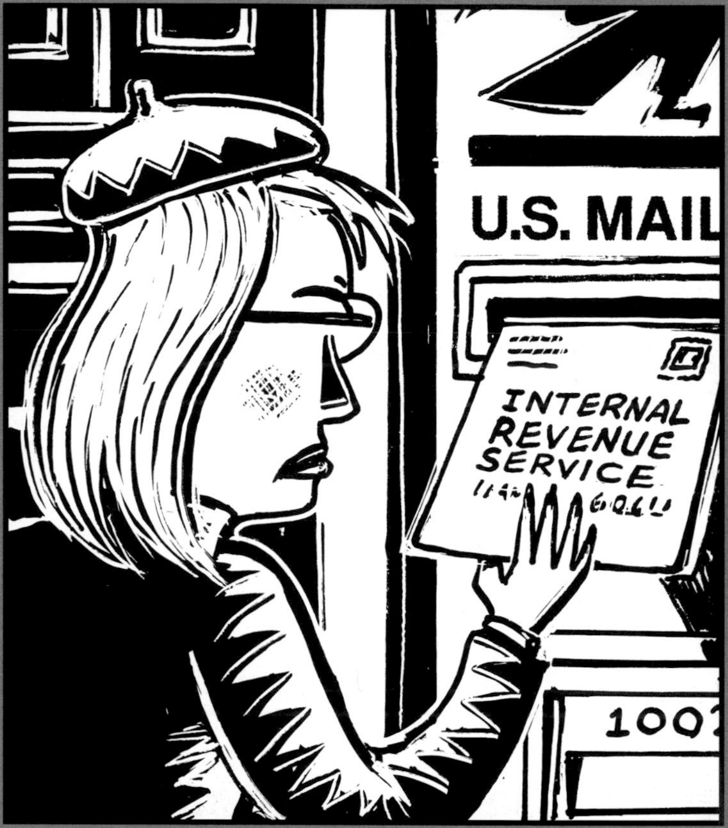
U.S. MAIL
INTERNAL
REVENUE
SERVICE

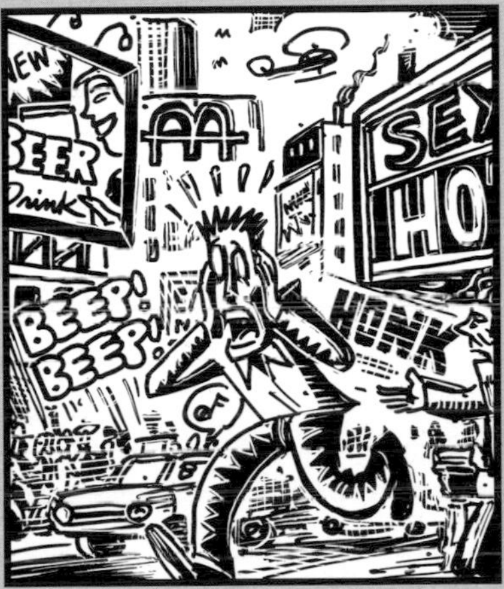
BEER
Drink
BEEP!
BEEP!
HONK

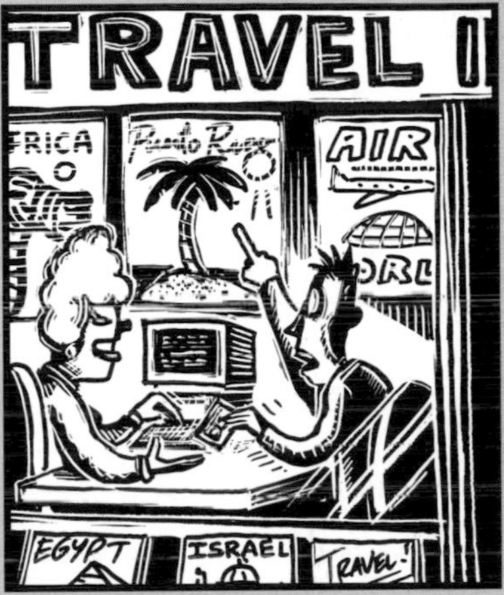
TRAVEL
Puerto Rico
AIR
EGYPT
ISRAEL
TRAVEL

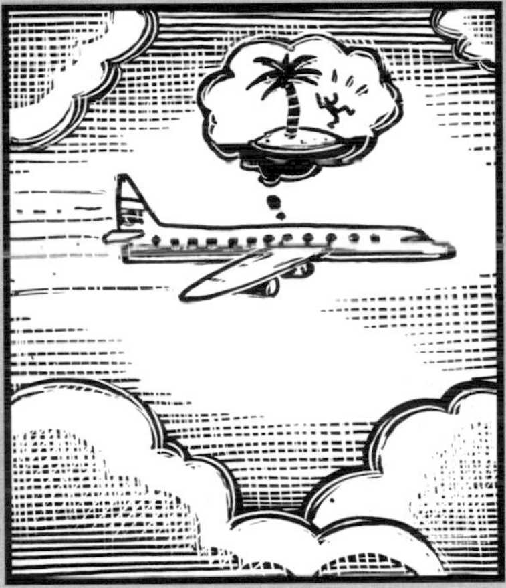

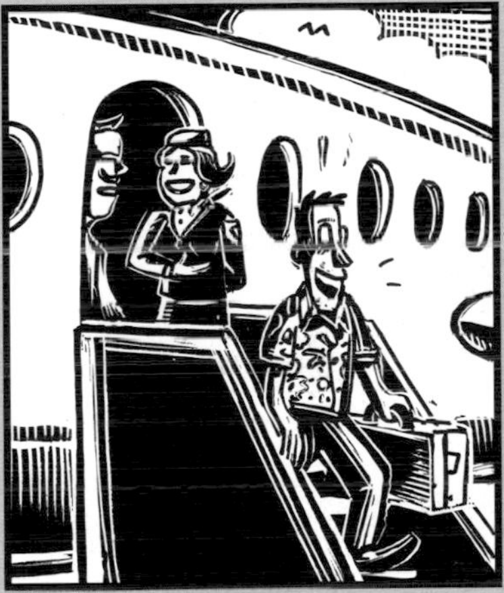

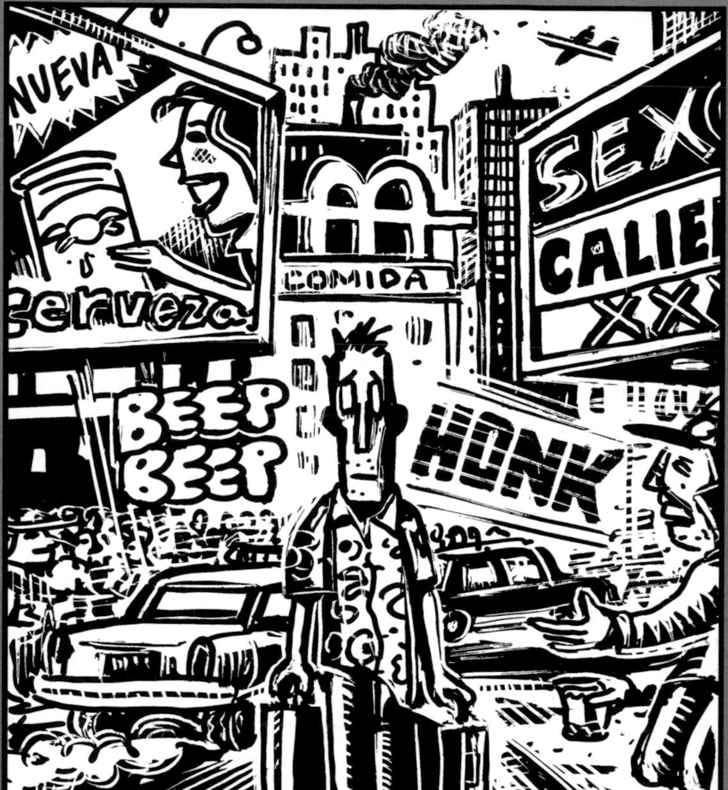
NUEVA
cerveza
COMIDA
BEEP
BEEP
HONK

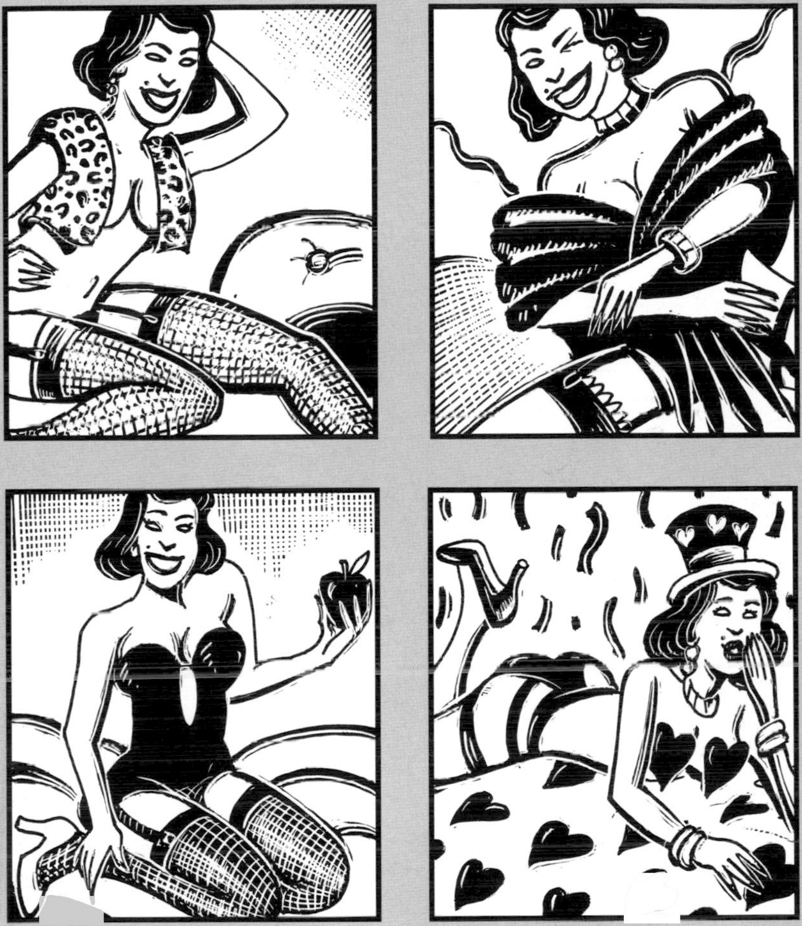

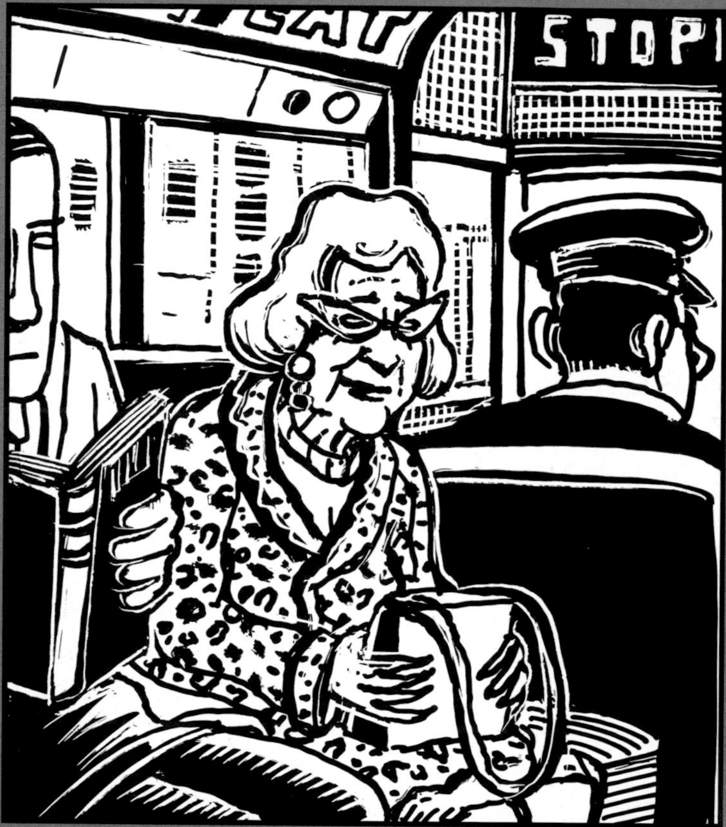
STOP

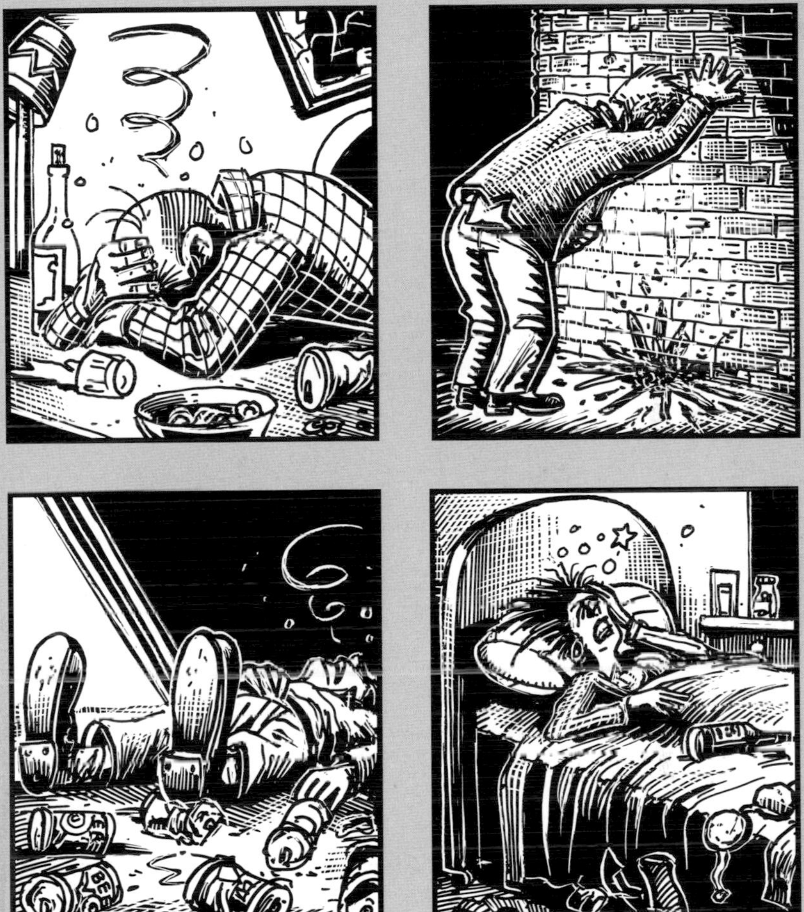

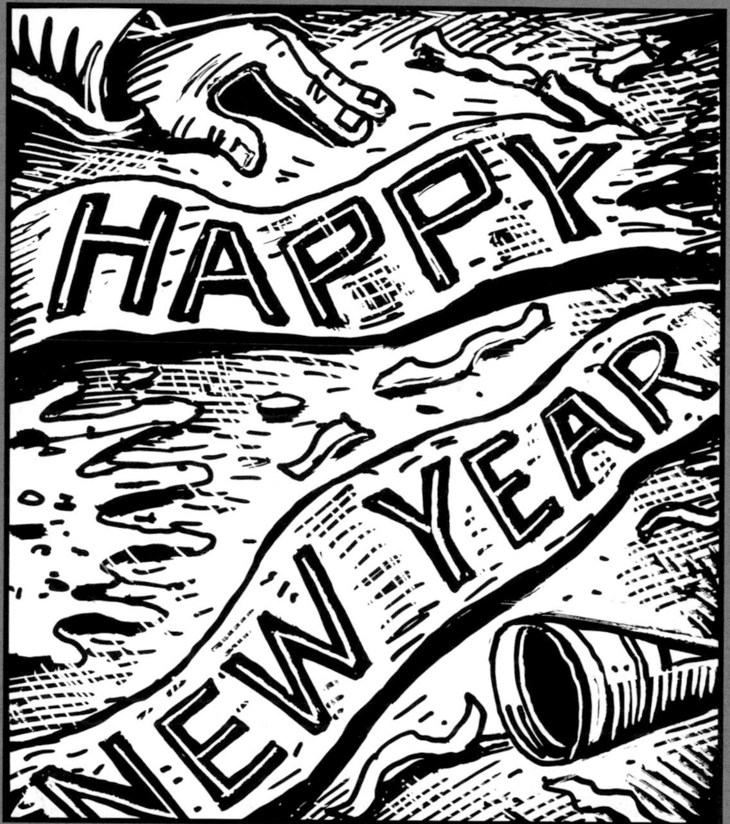
HAPPY
NEW YEAR

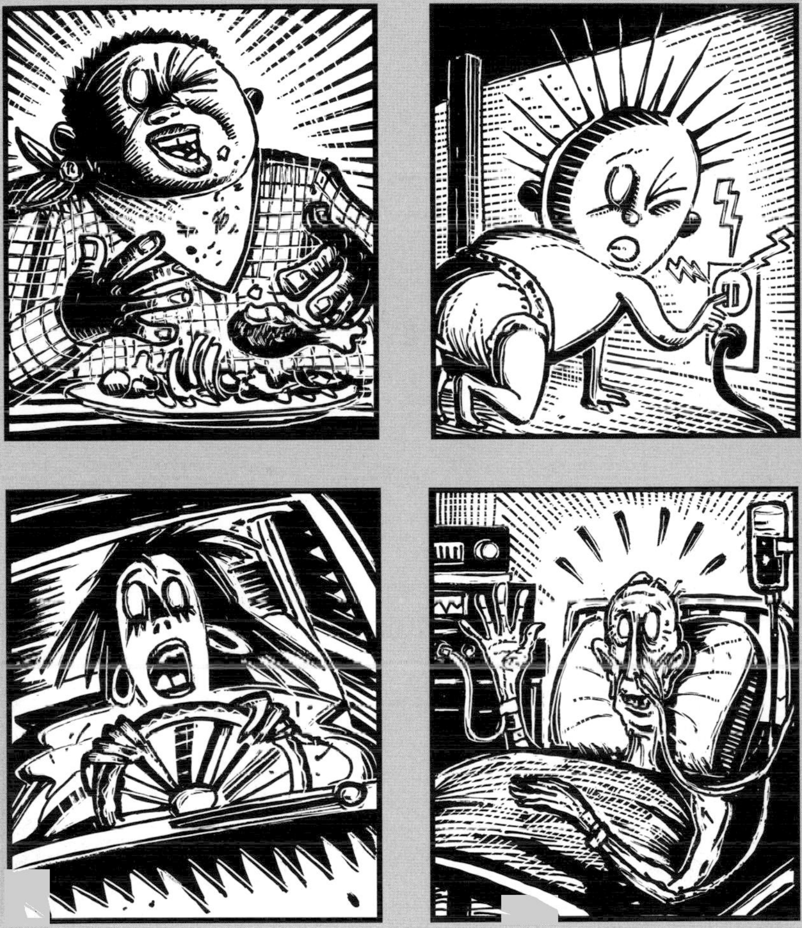

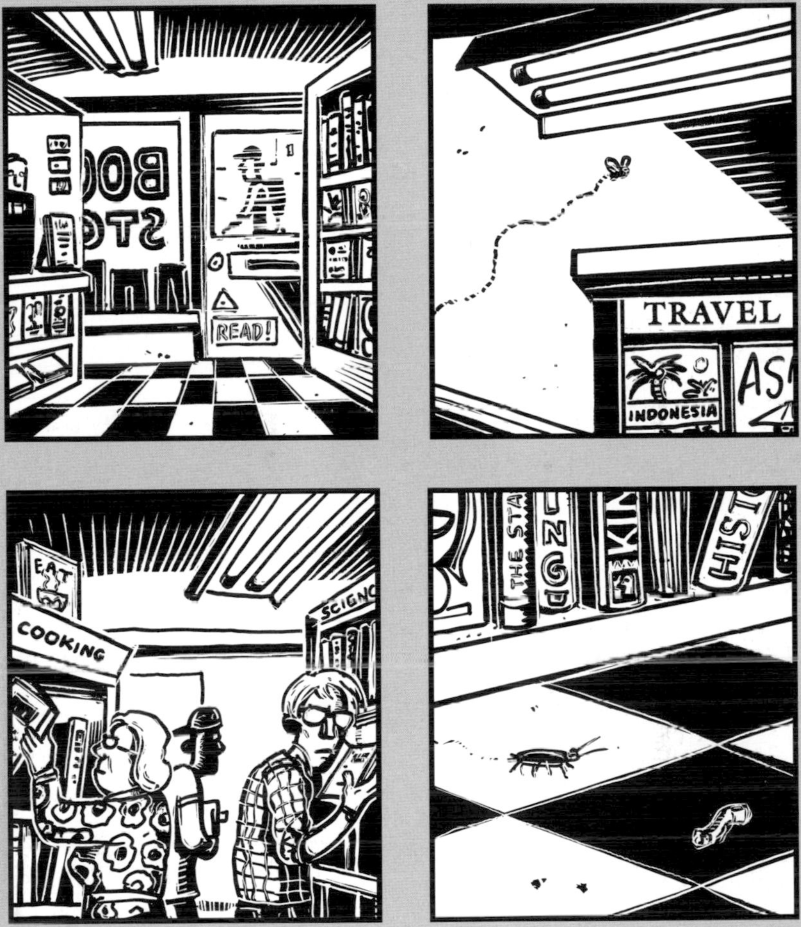
READ!
TRAVEL
INDONESIA
EAT
COOKING

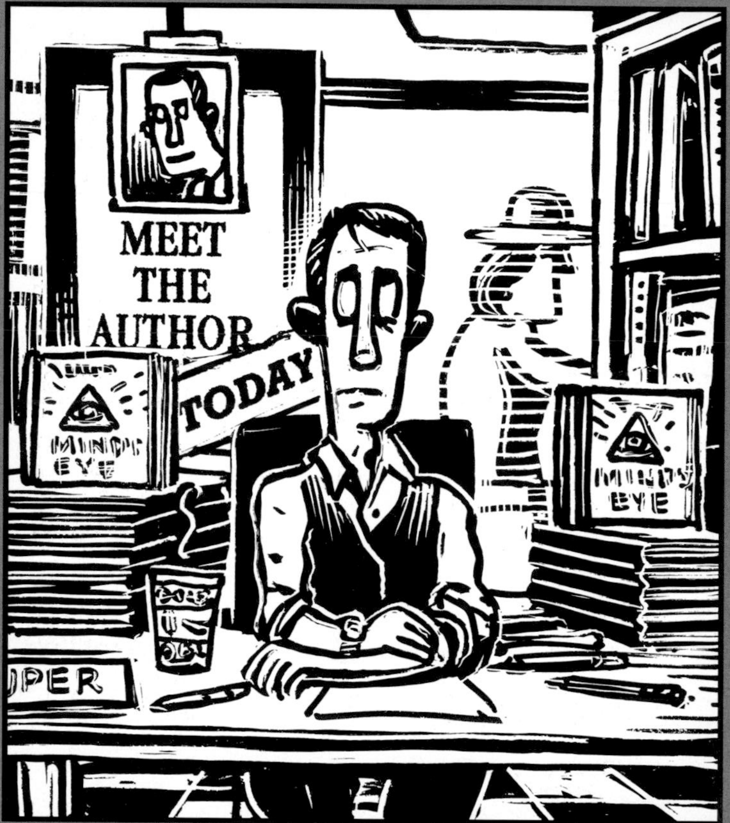
MEET
THE
AUTHOR
TODAY

ABOUT THE AUTHOR

Peter Kuper's comics and illustrations have appeared in *Time*, *Esquire*, *The New Yorker*, and *Mother Jones* among others. He co-founded the political magazine *World War 3 Illustrated* in 1979 and remains on the editorial board to this day. He is co-art director of *INX*, an editorial illustration group syndicated by United Feature, and produces a weekly comic strip for the New York Daily News Sunday Opinion Section. In 1996, he took over drawing "Spy vs. Spy" for *Mad Magazine*.

Peter resides in New York City with his wife Betty Russell and their daughter Emily.

ALSO BY THE AUTHOR

Eye of the Beholder
the first collection of the strip
(NBM)

Comics Trips
A journal of travel through
Africa and Southeast Asia
(NBM)

Give it Up!
and other short stories
by Franz Kafka
(NBM)

Stripped
An unauthorized autobiography
(Fantagraphics Books)

The System
(DC\Vertigo)

Speechless
Tales from the System
(Topshelf)

To see more, visit
www.peterkuper.com